AF484669

THE '80S PROJECT : 1980

JOSH
SPIEGEL

Josh Spiegel
Box Office Gold Productions
themovietimelinesguy@gmail.com

Youtube.com/@movietimeline

Thumb was just something special about the '80s when you're talking about movies, and even more so when you're talking about "genre" pictures. It's arguably the most important era for horror and sci-fi, with a large chunk of the output of the decade helping to define where their futures would lead.

Sure, the '30s were essentially the birthplace of horror, what with the Universal monsters rearing their heads.

Sure, the '50s would explode the sci-fi boom with the fear of technological advances and growing interest in space exploration.

Sure, the '70s would legitimize horror by allowing auteurs to dare to infuse a level of high art into their narratives and explore deeper themes.

But, none of those could touch the '80s. And there's threes reasons why. Number one is the development of cutting edge practical effects. Wizards like Tom Savini, Rick Baker, Rob Bottin, and dozens more would turn the world of special effects into a new magic show, delighting audiences with their visuals that would inspire new waves of "how did they do that?" Number two is the mass marketing of VHS players and the boom of video rental shops. After so many opened up, all looking to fill their shelves with product, there was a massive influx of interest in quick, cheap horror flicks to offer a selection. Finally, the third element was the easy access to camcorders. Filmmakers no longer needed extremely expensive camera equipment and thousands of dollars in film processing. All they needed was a video camera, some tapes, and their friends in the backyard.

I'm certainly not unique in saying that this decade holds a very special place in my heart for movies. I remember the video shops opening up nearby in my neighborhood, their racks holding so much mystery and intrigue. Insane box covers featuring people shackled to castle walls while a bloody meathook dangled in front of them, lumpy headed aliens with a machine gun in one hand and flipping me the bird with the other, and a severed robotic hand holding a chopping bag with a severed head in it. They called to me. For as much as I love the digital age of having access to pretty much anything I can think of, it doesn't quite match the feeling of walking into that video store, strolling into the horror/sci-fi section and scanning the covers, looking for some buried treasure of a spectacle. There was a certain amount of commitment required. It wasn't as simple as saying, "oh, I don't enjoy this," before clicking off and just finding something else. You had gone to the store. You picked the movies out. You had them for like, three days. Even if you had accidentally chosen the worst film known to man, you stuck with it. Or at least, I did.

The '80s Project is my effort to relive that wonder of unknowing. To relive the experience of the timeframe in which the films that shaped my infatuation with horror and sci-fi flourished. I decided to make an effort to watch all of the horror and sci-fi films released in the decade, in order of when they were released.

Now, for the sake of brevity, and let's face it, my sanity, i can't watch EVERYTHING. So I had to create some ground rules for how this would all work. First off, i eliminated short films. To get on the Project, it would have to be a feature length film. Secondly, i cast aside the vast majority of TV movies, although I chose to include some. Third, i had to get rid of some of the international entries, mainly due to just being irrelevant through an American perspective, but also due to availability. In order to watch them and include them here, I had to be able to find them, and let's face it, some of the more obscure Indonesian horror films aren't exactly at our fingertips. That being said, I didn't want to only stick to US theatrical releases, since that would eliminate a large number of important films. So I developed a fool proof system. I included them if I felt like it. I mainly stuck to things that

I felt were either important to horror/sci-fi cinema in general, or just to my own personal experiences of nostalgia.

This volume encompasses the releases of 1980/1981 that fall under the category of sci-fi, which in my opinion includes superhero films, fantasy, and even kaiju flicks. Each film entry will give you some detailed information about the film itself and the basic plot setup, although I've tried to keep spoilers or major plot twists out of it in order to preserve some mystery should you choose to seek these out for yourselves. I'll also give you my personal rating on each one, based on a five star system. I feel like I'm a bit stingy with my ratings, and reserve 5 stars for films that i consider the best of the best. They're pretty few, and far between. I will also rate the film based on a Cultural Significance, which I realize is a bit of an arbitrary rating, but I'll evaluate each film on how much of an impact it had on its specific genre. The interesting thing about that consideration is that it generally doesn't reflect my personal opinion on it. It may have had a massive impact on the film world, and yet not been a great film, or vice versa. The final rating each film will get is a simple recommendation. Sort of a "too long, didn't read" and will sum up each one with a suggestion to watch it, don't watch it, or maybe watch it. There's definitely films out there that I believe SHOULD be watched, even if they don't sound exactly like something that would be up one's alley, and also ones that I'm pretty confident that most people will not enjoy whatsoever. But there's a certain contingency of films that I know that some people will like, and others will not, so those will be the ones given the "maybes."

So, let's head into this decade and see what makes it so special, so radical, so tubular, and so worthy of all of the nostalgia that it gets draped upon it.

5

Jan 9th, '80
THE LATHE OF HEAVEN

The decade kicks off on January 9th with *The Lathe of Heaven*, which was actually a TV movie that ran on public television. It begins in Portlandia in what they say is the near future, and that evil Senator Kelly (Bruce Davidson) is here and he has a problem with taking pills and is sent to a doctor where he says his issue is the dreams that he's having. He's been abusing a number of prescription medications which he says have been helping to suppress his dreaming because, you see, George says that his dreams change reality. He claims that it has been that way since he was a mere 17 years old. He had a dream that a family member died in a car crash, and not only did it happen, but the details of their personal history were altered as well. The doc suggests a treatment of giving him a hypnotic suggestion for a positive dream, using the trigger word Antwerp, and refers to them as "effective dreams." He asks him to dream about a horse, which he does, altering a photo in the office, but making it so it had always been that way, so the doctor doesn't notice the change has happened. They try again, but this time, the doc actually witnesses the change taking place, and realizes George is telling the truth. Unfortunately, the doc decides that he can use George to improve the world, which just so happens to also make him much richer and more important. Along the way, he uses it to fight overpopulation by creating a plague to wipe out a large portion of humanity, stopping war by creating an alien invasion to unite humanity, and eliminating racism by making everyone grey. So, this was an adaptation of a popular novel of the same name from 1971, and actually was quite popular at the time, and was made for the low budget of a quarter of a million dollars. It was the very first made for TV movie for PBS, and would be aired for a while, but then was shelved due to a rights issue over a Beatles song that was featured in the film. At one point, George is given a recording of "With A Little Help From My Friends", and even references the song by name. The deal that was in place to use the song lasted for a short period of time, and after that deal expired, it was too expensive to renew and continue to use the recording. After a while, looking to rerelease the film, they decided that they only way they could do so was to remove the Beatles version, but the content of the lyrics was integral to the storyline. So, instead, they went a cheaper route and commissioned a cover version of the track, allowing for a DVD version to be released in 2000. It was remade in 2002, with James Caan as the doctor and Lukas Haas as George, but that version toned down the more fantastical elements, removing the aliens and the grey people and is still decent, but lacks the punch the original did.

My rating - 4. This is one that really appeals to me. When I think of science fiction, this is the precise type of film that I would generally think of. It's biggest interest seems to be developing its characters and the world that they inhabit, with the fantastic elements taking a bit of a back seat. As a social and political commentary, it works very well, with discussing some hot button topics that are still relevant today. Even with a low budget, it's still able to pull off some of the bigger concepts that it wants to, although I admit that they do look fairly cheap, particularly compared to some of the other films from the same era.

Cultural Significance - 2 This movie never really broke out into the main stream, and possibly even struggles to be considered a cult classic.

It's a bit of a lost treasure if anything. As such, its influence and significance is a bit lower on the scale. It gets a little extra boost based on the presence of a few name players.

Should you watch it? **Yes.** It's pretty damn good. If you're looking for a fast paced, sci-fi action film, it's not going to be what you're after, but if you're in the mood for a thoughtful, interesting character piece set in an every warping reality of circumstances, give it a shot.

Sequel? No

Remake? Yes.

QUICK RANK:

RATING -

CULTURAL SIGNIFICANCE -

8

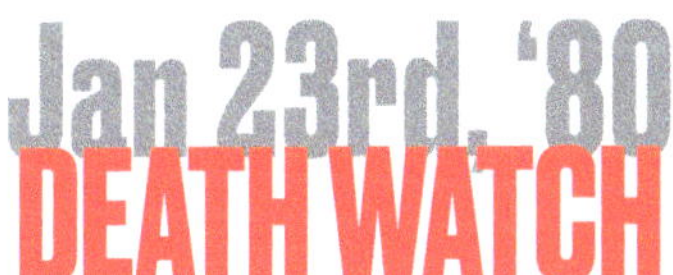

DEATH WATCH

Our next entry, *Death Watch*, premiered first in France, and took 2 more years to reach the United States, but it played world wide and festivals all throughout 1980. It features the Bad Lieutenant, Harvey Keitel, who undergoes an experimental surgery to implant a camera within his eyeball. With it, he is able to transmit everything he sees back to the television station that he works for, which is run by the Repo Man (Harry Dean Stanton). He gets a new assignment, his first with his new tech, and that's to follow Katherine, a woman with a terminal illness. In this near future society, diseases have been practically eliminated, so her condition is a bit of a rarity, making her of interest to the network. They have a new show that they're calling Death Watch, in which they plan to follow around a terminal patient during their final days, and Katherine is to be the primary subject. Sort of a more depressing *Truman Show*, in a way, where Truman dies at the end. After she realizes that she has no choice as to whether she'll be featured, she decides to scam the network and go on the lam. There's a rather brief appearance by Hagrid (Robbie Coltrane) as an agent of the show, and it would actually be his film debut, even if it's just for a moment or so. Roddy and his camera eye are sent after her, and he befriends her, filming in secret while he does. This one was directed by Bertrand Tavernier, a French filmmaker who was mostly known for straightforward dramas, and a sci-fi film was out of his normal zone, but it would partially predict the future of television and the interest in reality shows that would follow around regular people. *The Truman Show* comparisons continue in the way that she is being televised without being aware of it. Later on in the film, Ming the Merciless (Max Von Sydow) shows up to play Katherine's former husband, and this is not the only time we'll be seeing

him this year, and he rounds out a very solid cast list. Upon release, it was fairly successful, but not largely so, especially considering the talent involved. There is an extra footnote concerning the film that's a bit of a sad note. There's a sequence in a park, and one of the children playing is David Schneider, son of the film's lead actress, Romy Schneider. About one year after the film's release, David was killed in a horrible accident killing him at the age of 14. The loss took its toll on Romy, and she went into a deep depression. In 1982, she was found dead in her apartment, the victim of a cardiac arrest. It's possible that the death was a suicide by means of alcohol and sleeping pills, but there's no definite conclusions there.

My Rating - 3.
This is a pretty damn interesting concept and great character study, but it definitely suffers a bit as it goes on. The setup for the film is great, and the world that it defines is one where you would want to spend more time. However, the script seems more interested in getting the characters out into the countryside, away from all those elements, and it eventually plummets into a bit of a cliched finale. The best aspect of the film is that, like *Black Mirror*, it isn't necessarily about the science fiction elements, and they are merely a backdrop for the story elements. Instead of giving us a sci-fi tale, we're treated to a dramatic tale in a sci-fi world, and given some full fledged characters to follow.

Cultural Significance - 2.5.
This one is interesting because it does feature familiar faces and led to further explorations of technological intrusions into our lives, but the film itself isn't really remembered or discussed, or even given credit for those things. In the end, it just didn't leave enough of an impact.

Should you watch it? Absolutely. There's great themes being explored, and even if I think it doesn't stick the landing, it's worth the (death) watch.

Sequel? No.

Remake? No.

On Valentine's Day, the world was given a gift, because In Italy, The *Pumaman* was born. This kicks off with a text crawl that informs us that long ago, Aztec gods came to Earth to create the first Pumaman, a protector for our world. They take the form of a glowing ball and leave a golden mask, before it jumps to modern day. Doc

Loomis (Donald Pleasance) is here although in this film, he has a penchant for garish leather outfits. He's the villainous Mr. Kobras, and he's on the hunt for the Pumaman, and a lot has been said about his pronunciation. He emphasizes the first syllable to say "Pyewma man" and this has been a source of ridicule of the film. However, considering that is the British pronunciation of the word "puma," it wasn't as if that was a choice that the actor made. Kobras has been sending his men to find the hero, throwing those that he suspects out of windows. We're then introduced to a man named Vadinho, who throws our main character, Tony, out a window, so you would believe that he was responsible for the other deaths. But, when Tony survives, revealed to have the power of Pumaman, Vadinho states that he is not responsible for the other window incidents, and he knew that Tony was Pumaman all along, and would survive the fall. It's all…confusing. Pumaman's power set includes a danger detection ability, enhanced fighting skills, and night vision, and gets a superhero costume in the final act, although it more resembles a set of pajamas. Interestingly, Walter George Alton, who plays Tony, only acted in one other film before quitting acting to become a prominent partner for a medical malpractice firm in New York, and was once interviewed on the Daily Show. Our hero adds flight to his skill set, although the effects for it are delightfully low budget, although for an Italian feature, the price tag was more mid level. Even with some of the special effects being silly looking, it actually did have a handful of nice practical work, including Pumaman bursting through walls, and destroying bricks on the side of a building as he tries to grab on to them. Unfortunately, it was a bust at the box office, failing to make any impact, although over time, it's developed a form of infamy. Donald Pleasance would refer to it as the worst film that he appeared in, and think about that statement. Take a second to check out that man's filmography and think to yourself, "THIS was what he thought was the worst one?" Even the director would distance himself, claiming he only made it in order to cash in on current trends, and that financial issues during production kept it from being the movie that he wanted. All of that amounted to cult success, due to its reputation of being a terrible film, with the MST3K guys giving it their riffing treatment, opening it up to a new audience.

My Rating - 2.5. There's a certain charm here, and it's pretty easy to see how people would lump this one into a sort of "so bad that it's good" category, but the truth is that it doesn't quite make up enough of the film. In between those goofball moments, there's rather long lulls in the action that grind everything to a halt, and it perhaps takes a a little too long for Pumaman to show up in all of his costumed glory. Pleasance is a treat, though, and could stand to be in the film a little more, considering that Alton is a touch of a bore as the lead, and it's not hard to see why he ended up leaving the business.

Cultural Significance - 1.5. This one has a pretty low rating here, because outside of the presence of Pleasance, there not much that stands out here. Were it

not for its growing status of being a bit of guilty pleasure cinema, it likely would be completely forgotten. Even his powers are a bit derivative and simply end up being lower budgeted versions of abilities that we've already seen.

Should You Watch It? Perhaps watch the riffed version to get some extra laughs, but in its standard form, it's fairly skippable.

Sequel? No.

Remake? No.

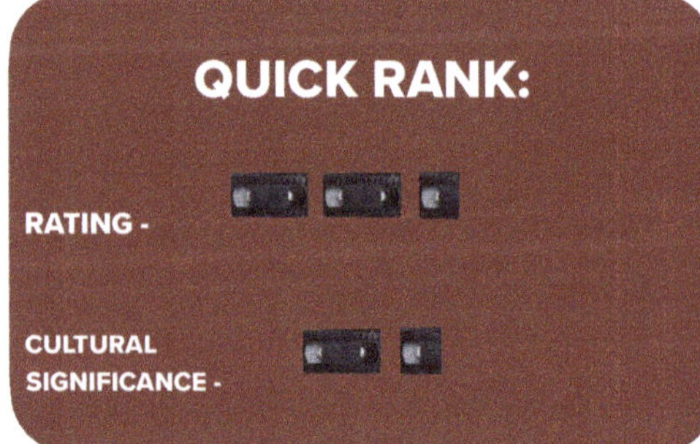

Feb 15th, '80
SATURN 3

One day later, on the 15th, *Saturn 3* was released, the highest profile sci-fi film of the year so far. The opening of the film contains one of the more gruesome effects of 1980, with a man being launched out into space. The intense cold of the vacuum freezes his body instantly, so when he crashes into parts of the ship, he explodes into a number of bloody, frozen pieces. A man then hijacks a ship and takes it to Saturn's third moon, the Saturn 3 of the title, and the man is revealed to be Harvey Keitel, for his second appearance this year. There, he encounters Spartacus (Kirk Douglas) and Angel (Farrah Fawcett), but as soon as he opens his mouth, you realize that something is off. It seems that after filming was complete, they didn't really think that Keitel's New York accent worked for the character or the film, so they decided to change it. Stories vary, but he was either unavailable at the time and couldn't do it, or was insulted at the prospect of redoing the audio and refused to do it. Instead, they brought in esteemed character actor, Roy Dotrice, to dub over his voice. Captain Benson is revealed to be rather unstable, and has brought along a robot that runs off of pure brain tissue that is meant to take one of their places there. That robot was a massive special effect dubbed Hector that took twenty people to animate and cost a million dollars. It was a very complicated animatronic and comes with the ability to make me uncomfortable with a scene in which it extracts a small splinter from Alex's eyeball. But, the most interesting aspect of this film is the

behind the scenes drama, which went well beyond the swapping out of Keitel's brash tones. It was originally supposed to be directed by John Barry, the Oscar winning Art Director who worked on *Star Wars, Superman, A Clockwork Orange*, and tons of others, and this was meant to be his directorial debut. However, very early on during shooting, Stanley Donan, one of the film's producers, realized that things weren't exactly going to plan. Kirk Douglas exhibited some ego flare ups, constantly butting heads with the director, and the shoot just wasn't working, so Barry was eventually fired. Now, there's a couple of different versions of what went down, because it's said that he was outright fired, and that Douglas took over directing for a day or two, but Donan says the Barry was never fired. He claims that when things started going awry, he insisted on being on set every day to make sure that the production went smoothly, which Barry objected to, and walked off set and never returned. However it happened, he was off the film, and then immediately moved on to so second unit directing on the *Empire Strikes Back*, and while working there, collapsed on set and died of meningitis. After Barry left, Donan took over as the director, a role that he had performed dozens of times before, but for very different kinds of film, like *Singing In The Rain* and *Seven Brides For Seven Brothers*. According to the cast, when he came on board, everything changed, including major

aspects of the story. And, whereas Barry feuded with Douglas, Donan couldn't get along with Keitel, causing the actor to refer to the movie as the worst moment of this entire career. And in the end, it all fell apart, since it was bashed by critics, and was a major bust at the box office, bringing in only 9 million dollars against a 10 million dollar budget, and became a bit of an embarrassment for the cast afterwards. In fact, the film's screenwriter, Martin Amis, went on to make a book based on the making of *Saturn 3*. He would change the names and finer details in order to separate it a bit, but it's pretty clear that it was based on these events.

My Rating - 3.5. I understand that this is not that good, and has its issues, but I enjoy it anyway. Part of that might be nostalgia, since I saw this film quite a bit when I was younger, and my taste for finer script elements wasn't "refined," but I also can't help being in awe of the amazing effects behind the Hector bot. It's great to see in action, and the more extreme elements stick out in my head. It's hard to call it fun, since the plot takes itself seriously, although the camp elements show through. The weirdest part, and the hardest thing to swallow, is the love story between Adam and Alex, considering there was a 31 year age gap between the two actors. It's accommodated for in the plot, though, as Alex has grown up on the moon, and encountered few other people, but it doesn't really make it any less odd to see.

Cultural Significance - 3.5. This has more clout since it is well remembered, though it's mostly for the wrong reasons. Besides that, it has an impressive cast list, featuring some of the bigger names of the time, was sort of the last mark on the industry from John Barry, and contained the innovation of the Hector bot.

Should You Watch It? Yes. I would recommend giving it a shot, even just for the aspect of seeing a disaster play out on screen.

Sequel? No

Remake? No

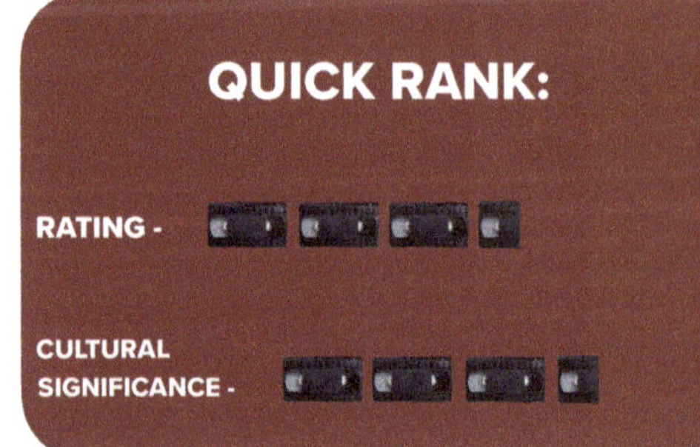

SIMON

The final film of February is a little number called *Simon*, although its exact release date isn't known. The cast list is huge, with character actor Austin Pendleton as a scientist and his team of Willie Tanner (Max Wright), the Phantom of the Paradise (William Finley), and Dr. Van Dongen who probably

means no harm, but he's really very short on charm, since he's played by Wallace Shawn. Their group wants to test out a psychological experiment in which they'll convince the world that an alien has landed on earth, so they recruit a local college professor, played by Peevey (Alan Arkin), and tell him that they think he's a genius. Next, Lili Von Shtup (Madeline Kahn) pops in and they team her up with him, and then place him into a prolonged stint of sensory deprivation. This causes him to lose it a bit, and he goes through his approximation of the scope of human evolution, in a scene that's somewhat reminiscent of *Altered States*, a film that will give a more serious take on the same subject later on this year. In this particular time frame, there was a big interest in sensory deprivation and its effects, so it's not really surprising to see that reflected in multiple films. Part of their experiment goes according to plan, since Simon is soon convinced that he's actually an alien that was left behind on Earth as a child, and when he's announced to the media, he becomes a huge sensation worldwide. Unfortunately, Simon has some pretty wild ideas for how the world should work, and when he starts to share his bold opinions, he takes away the spotlight from the scientists. Later on in the film, Jud Crandall (Fred Gwynne) shows up for a bit, and interestingly, about 12 years later he would go on to share the screen with Pendleton again in the comedy classic, *My Cousin Vinny*. This one was directed by Marshall Brickman, who was mostly know for writing, and his work with Woody Allen. This is the man who won an Oscar for Annie Hall, and another for Manhattan,

and also wrote Allen's Sleeper, which shared a similar to to this one. But, outside of a single TV episode, this was his first directorial work, and would remain one of only three films that he took that role in his entire career. Upon initial release, it would split opinions across the board. It did fairly well at the box office, bringing in $6 million, although there's no budget information to compare that to. However, considering that comedies of the era were notoriously inexpensive, and the sci-fi elements of the film were fairly meager, it's hard to imagine that the price tag was that high.

My Rating - **2.5**. This one is almost a 3 for me, but not quite there. If I were doing quarters, I would consider this a 2.75 or something, but I'm not doing that, so a 2.5 it is. The problem is that with as much leeway as I tend to give trashy horror, I am not so forgiving with comedy. And in this one, some of the humor lands, but the vast majority of the jokes fall flat. It's an interesting thing to view this in comparison to the Allen films that he worked on as well, because you can see some similarities, but it's clear how much that the collaboration mattered. The concepts that it keeps bringing up are interesting, but on the whole, it just doesn't work.

Cultural Significance - **2.5.** This is one that you would think would have a little more significance, considering the sheer number of

recognizable faces within, but ended up still going under the radar. I think that it's entirely possible that this has one of the largest ratios of name value to film notoriety that I can think of. This lineup, in any other circumstances, would probably be considered a slam dunk, but instead, this has somehow slipped into obscurity.

Should You Watch It? Probably. But I suppose your enjoyment may vary depending on if you were interested in the comedy aspects versus the sci-fi ones.

Sequel? No

Remake? No

QUICK RANK:

RATING -

CULTURAL SIGNIFICANCE -

Mar 15th, 80
THE FORBIDDEN ZONE

This next entry is a real doozy, because on March 15th, in Los Angeles, there was the premiere of *The Forbidden Zone*, although it wouldn't get a wider release until two years later, in 1982. The opening theme is by Oingo Boingo, very early on in their career, and that's because this film was directed by band leader Danny Elfman's brother, Richard. The story concerns the Hercules family, which includes Frenchy, played by Richard's then wife, Marie Pascale-Elfman. They're a bizarre mish mash of a family, living in a black and white world that occasionally becomes a musical, incorporating classic songs from Cab Calloway and others. It also sometimes shifts into stop motion animation and traditional animation. After discovering a doorway to the sixth dimension in their basement, Frenchy accidentally falls in, where she encounters a laundry list of strange characters. There's the King, played by Tattoo (Herve Villechaize), and his queen, Ramona Ricketts (Susan Tyrrell), as well as the bizarre art duo, the Kipper Kids, and a heavy set man wearing Mickey Mouse ears lip synching a song. It's a strange moment in the film, made stranger by the behind the scenes story. Seems the actor was from Richard's neighborhood and who wanted to be in the movie. However, when they got on set, he froze up, and in order to make use of the footage, they ended up superimposing the lips directly onto him, creating a surreal, humorous moment. The cast also included Matthew Bright, who was a part of Elfman's theater troupe, and would then go on to direct the Reese Witherspoon movie, *Freeway*, but then also made the most confusing film of all time, *Tiptoes*. Elfman was able to cast Tyrrell through a mutual connection, but she brought Villechaize on board, as the two were a couple in real life at the time. Along the way, there would also be quick appearances from Andy Warhol ingenue, Viva, and the Maniac, Joe Spinell, but would also feature Oingo Boingo themselves, with Danny Elfman appearing as the devil. When it first debuted, it didn't perform all that well, and some of the more offensive aspects of the film were criticized, with some being accurate and others, not so much. People complained about one of the characters being an over the top Jewish stereotype, but the role was actually filled by Elfman's own grandfather, who says that cartoonish portrayal was how he was in real life. Over the next couple of decades, it would become a bizarre cult relic, with most of the attention being drive by the curiosity of Danny Elfman's involvement. For years, they tried to get a sequel off the ground, and ran a successful crowdfunding campaign in 2014, but nothing has materialized as of yet.

My Rating - 4. Wow. I just love this so, so much. I can very clearly remember seeing this for the first time, and not understanding what it was that I was seeing. It just felt so chaotic and unlike anything that I had ever seen before, but I knew that it was for me. I fully understand that it doesn't make much sense and that some of the elements just didn't age that well, but everything is so over the top that it's hard to take it seriously enough to consider offensive. And not only is it a visual treat, with an assortment of cool low budget, innovative film techniques going on, but it's just a delight for the ears as well. The music in this film is top notch, and it's probably one of the most underrated soundtracks of all time. I mean, it's got Oingo Boingo and Cab Calloway tunes intermixed, so it's a slam dunk all around.

Cultural Significance - 2.5. This is another one where I would love to rank this one higher, but because it never really made an impact at the time, and is still seen as a sort of weird cult oddity, I just can't justify it. It does hold some significance though, since it technically launched Danny Elfman's scoring career, and featured a cast list that wouldn't be out of place on the *Doctor Demento* show.

Should You Watch It? Absolutely. Keep in mind that some of the humor falls under the tasteless category, though, but it's a ride that you won't regret.

Sequel? No, damn it. Hurry up with that.

Remake? No

QUICK RANK:

RATING -

CULTURAL SIGNIFICANCE -

GAMERA : SUPER MONSTER

Ok. This next one is weird, because in Japan, on March 20th, the final Showa era Gamera film was released. Over there, it had the name *Uchu Kaiju Gamera*, or *Space Monster Gamera*, but would get an American release a few months later, in May, where it would be retitled *Gamera : Super Monster*. There's several reasons why this one was so strange, the first being that the last film in the series had been in 1971, 9 years earlier, and the character was only brought out of retirement in an effort to get Daiei, the company with the Gamera rights, out of a tight spot financially. The story would involve an alien warlord named Zanon coming to invade Earth, but is opposed by a trio of superheroines, which is the 2nd reason why this is unusual. There have never been any super powered individuals in the Gamera universe up until this point, but here it's played off like they've been around for quite a while. Zanon's plan involves unleashing the Gyaos, the villain from one the earlier Gamera films, so the friend to all children has to take him on. However, if you're a fan with the series, the fight will look extremely familiar, because all of the footage is lifted from 1967's *Gamera vs. Gyaos*. After he defeats the flying villain, in exactly the same way he did earlier, because it's the same scenes as before, he's forced to fight Zigra from 1971's *Gamera vs. Zigra*, and again, it's just reused footage. All of the fight scenes, and in fact, every single bit of footage that includes our giant turtle friend is just stock scenes, lifted wholesale from the other entries. But, the thievery doesn't stop there. Some of the space shots, featuring the invading ships and such, were taken from other Japanese films, some animated, including *Space Battleship Yamato* and *Galaxy Express 999*. Basically, only the

scenes with the human kid and the superhero trio were shot specifically for the film, making up about 25 percent of the total runtime, which made it a very inexpensive film to produce. There are a few short clips with Gamera that were exclusive to this film, though, including a scene where the big turtle knocks over a board advertising a Godzilla film, which is actually the closest thing to an onscreen crossover that we ever got. When everything was said and done, though, the film was unsuccessful, earning no money, and forcing Daiei into bankruptcy shortly afterwards. This was seen as the end of the character, and he'd go on the shelf, not to return for 15 years, which means that we won't encounter the big guy again until the '90s Project.

My Rating - 1.5. I'm a Gamera fan. There's just something about a giant, flying turtle that shoots rocket blasts in order to spin around that tickles me. So, you can imagine my disappointment with the equivalent of one of those sitcom clip show episodes where the cast gets stuck in a fridge or something. I had seen all of the films that the footage here was pulled from, so just being shown it again, with some really cheap additional stuff tossed in between, yeah, i wasn't having that. If this were any one, and i mean any one, of the original films, you can guarantee my rating would be much higher, and a low score isn't indicative of the one i would give the features that this footage came from. In fact, I'd give any one of those films a much higher rating, but i just can't extrapolate that into this film, a half hearted retread of those.

Cultural Significance - 2. The significance here is pretty low, since it's absolutely the least important film for Gamera. He's not even in the film except for the recycled footage. The only reason that it's getting a 2 here, instead of a 1, is that it's the final entry of the Showa era, and the only appearance of our terrapin friend for the entire decade.

Should You Watch It? - Absolutely not. If you want to see the big guy, just stick to the main entries, instead of this clip show format.

Sequel? Not in this era. Instead, the 90's would see a full on reboot.

Remake? Not of this entry.

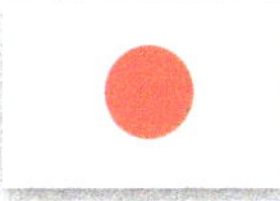

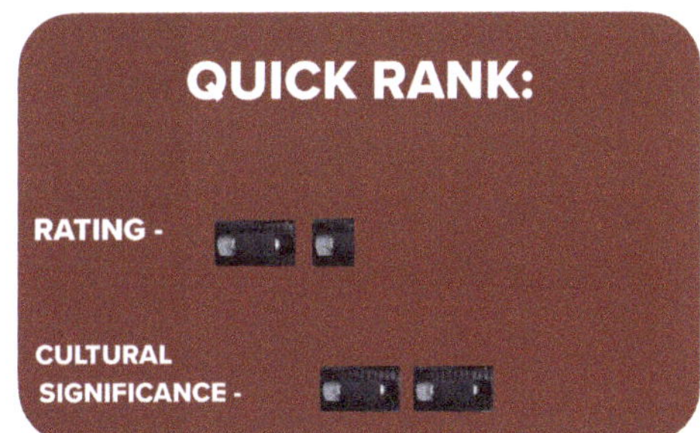

June 6th, '80
GALAXINA

Next up, we'll head deeper in space for the somewhat notorious *Galaxina*, which arrived on June 6th. It starts off with a blatant parody of the *Star Wars* text crawl, telling us that it's the year 3008, and informs us about a police cruiser ship called the Infinity. There's then another Lucas parody, with that opening ship shot,

showing an extended view of a massive space ship passing overhead, and that seemed to be a recurring theme among the science fiction films of 1980. The captain of the Infinity is cleverly named Cornelius, uh…Butt, and on board is Sean's dad from *Monster Squad* (Steven Macht), and a lovely robot named Galaxina, played by the 1980 Playboy Playmate of the Year, Dorothy Stratten. The captain himself is played by a face you've seen a million times, and yet don't know the name of. That name is Avery Schroeder, and although he's never landed big roles, he was in basically everything and also does about a million voices for cartoons, although sadly, based on his appearance and facial hair, it's a crime that he was never cast Mario. Plus, I've never really thought of Macht as any sort of, like, hunky guy, but apparently the filmmakers did, since he's featured shirtless quite a bit here. The Infinity also has a pretty cool practical creature in their brig known as Rockeater, as well as shipmates Sam and Maurice. I think that Maurice is supposed to resemble a Vulcan, but he's clearly not, since he has also bat wings on his back. Galaxina somewhat serves as the ship's maid, but she's definitely not a sex bot, since if they try to touch her, they get a shock. When Butt eats one of Rockeater's eggs, for some reason, he spits up a baby alien in a scene that I think could be spoofing something, I'm sure I'll think of what it is eventually. Otherwise, there's just not a lot of plot here, and it's instead a series of wacky set pieces, written and directed by William Sachs, the director of the schlock classic, *The Incredible Melting Man*. He hasn't really directed that many films, but had one out every year or two before this, but afterwards, took a couple of five year gaps in between projects, with his final work being a family film in 2001. The crew goes to the equivalent of the Star Wars cantina, where they encounter an assortment of aliens in silly masks, and a woman with 3 boobs, years before that was done in *Total Recall*.

There's also a very brief appearance by a woman doing a robot dance, who may or may not be intended to be a robot, played by the lovely Rhonda Shear from the classic USA series, *UP All Night*. But, the real thing to talk about here is Galaxina herself. Stratten had previously acted in small things here and there, and even filmed one more project after this one, but *Galaxina* premiered in June of '80, and two months later, in August, her estranged husband murdered her and then committed suicide. It put a permanent stain on the film and made it forever linked to that tragedy, which is a shame because even with a limited role and playing a robot, she's pretty great here. There's also fun special FX and monsters, but sadly, it's a comedy that's not that funny, with obvious humor like Mr. Spot, who is simply just Mr. Spock

with bigger ears, and it can't seem to decide if it wants to be a parody or not. Even though the film premiered in June, it went wide in August, the day after Stratten was killed. When news of her death hit, *Galaxina* was yanked out of theaters, and they waited a few months before attempting to release it again. It was then met with a bit of controversy and negative reviews, causing it to be considered a financial and artistic failure.

My Rating - **2.5**. When it comes to movies, particularly bad movies, I have a level of tolerance. When it comes to horror movies, I feel like that tolerance level is damn high. With comedies however, my patience can run really thin, really quickly. And *Galaxina* tries so hard to be funny, and every time it does, it manages to kill every ounce of good will it had built until that point. There's plenty to enjoy, because the premise is fun, and the talent involved is great, and it's people I've seen handle comedy before, and handle it well. So, I feel I have to partially blame the direction of Sachs, and consider that comedy may not have been his forte. As evidenced by *The Incredible Melting Man*, he was capable of creating some unintentional comedy, but when he's TRYING to make you laugh…not so capable. I did like Stratten, and any scene with her and Macht interacting stole the show, and I almost wish the central story focused on them instead of trying to be an ensemble.

Cultural Significance -

3. It's hard to deny that this film has a certain place in the genre's history, but it's an unintended one. The death of Stratten will always hang over this one, and remains the thing that it's most known for. However, the film itself does have a few other things to mention. It has a collection of cool effects, some recognizable faces, and the cinematography is by *The Thing*'s Dean Cundy.

Should You Watch It?

That probably depends on how much you can handle bad comedy. If sitting through joke after joke not landing sounds like complete torture, then you're going to want to skip this.

Sequel? No.

Remake? No.

QUICK RANK:

RATING -

CULTURAL SIGNIFICANCE -

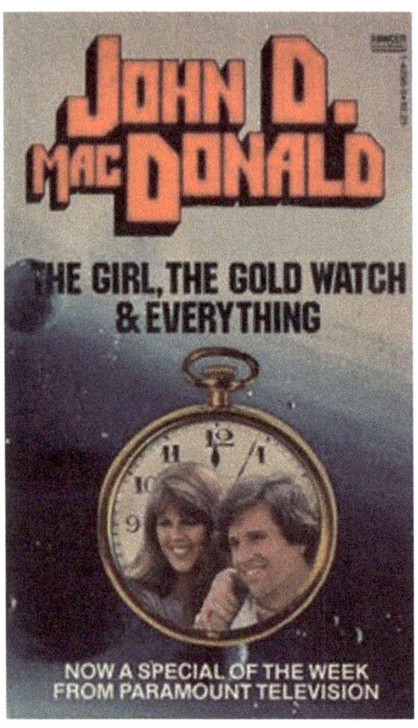

We're moving back onto the small screen on June 13th, since there was a TV movie called *The Girl, The Gold Watch, And Everything*. It starts off with a super peppy opening theme song that feels like it should be the credits to a sitcom, and then introduces Ted Striker (Robert Hays). Maurice Evans also appears here, although it's a bit strange to see him without his Dr. Zaius ape makeup. In the story, when Kirby's rich uncle dies, he doesn't leave him anything except for a gold pocket watch, which seems like a bit of a bummer, especially when some sort of a tax snafu leaves him stuck working for his uncle's company at a pretty low rate of pay. There's then this oddball brother and sister team who appear to be taking advantage of Kirby, but are also looking for something, and things get worse for him when he finds out that he's being charged with embezzlement by the company. The devious Charla is played by Jill Ireland, who is most known for being in one of the *Death*

Wish films, since she was married to Charles Bronson, and remained so until her passing in 1990 from breast cancer. Then, 40 minutes into the movie, Mindy (Pam Dawber) shows up, doing some kind of accent that I can't quite figure out. I think it's supposed to be Texan, or some sort of generalized southern twang, but I'm not sure she pulls it off. She's introduced as she comes into Kirby's room at night, mistakes him for someone else and has sex with him. When she realizes he's not who she thought he was, she's freaked out, but then they talk for about 10 minutes and she realizes that she's in love with him,

so it's all okay. And then, a full 50 minutes into this 90 minute movie, he finally activates the gold watch and discovers that it can freeze time. Contrary to most movies that have this conceit, his first instinct is not to enter into the women's locker room, but when Bonnie tries it out, the first thing that she does is take people's clothes off. The director here was William Wiard, who did a ton of TV and TV movies, including *This House Possessed* from 1981.

My Rating - 2. There's a ton of promise in this premise, and yet everything is just glossed over so quickly. The very concept of having a watch that can stop time seems to offer a ton of options for fun scenarios and narrative shenanigans. And yet, this movie takes advantage of exactly zero of that promise. The very fact that no one even activates the watch until the movie is more than half over is extremely frustrating, and we're left with a series of vaguely comedic setups that don't really go anywhere while we wait. The only thing that really saves it are Hays and Dawber, because goofy accent or no, they're both really charming and carry their characters well.

popular enough to earn a sequel. In terms of contributions to the genre, it barely qualifies since it seems to constantly forget its science fiction elements. There is a handful of familiar faces, however, and that's enough to bump it up the extra point five.

Should You Watch It? You can probably pass on this one. It's not really dramatic enough to back up its premise.

Sequel? Yes. One year later, *The Girl, The Gold Watch, and Dynamite* was released. It carries on the story of Kirby and Bonnie, although most of the roles would be recast.

Remake? No.

Cultural Significance - **1.5**. As far as TV movies go, this one is pretty lost in the shuffle, although it was

June 20th, '80

THE EMPIRE STRIKES BACK

We're headed back out in space now, and this next film came out on June 20th, and it's a little indie film that you possibly may have heard of, called *The Empire Strikes Back*. This picks up after the events of *Star Wars : A New Hope*, and takes us to the ice planet of Hoth. There, we get some outstanding sequences with the Tauntaun, the Wampa creature, and then that fantastic battle with the giant AT-AT Imperial Walkers and let me tell you. Every single child of 1980 was envious of the kids that got one of those under their tree at Christmas time. It's kind of hard to reflect on this now, due to the immense amount of tampering with the visuals in later releases, but just know that even the original effects were extremely damn impressive for 1980, and when you compare the level of effect of this film to … well…anything else in this book from the same year, and it's mind blowing that it's from the same time frame. Now, I think that the general public is under the assumption that George Lucas directed the entire original trilogy. I mean, I know that *Star Wars* fans know that he didn't, but your average guy on the street thinks so, but *Empire* was actually directed by Irvin Kershner, which seems like an odd choice if you look at his filmography, since there's not much similar on there. He had previous done more lightweight fare, including some comedies, and the occasional western, but Lucas knew him and trusted him. Kershner almost said no, though, because coming on to direct the sequel to such a popular film was daunting, but ultimately he said yes. After this, he would only make 2 more theatrical films, directing the quasi-Bond film, *Never Say Never Again*, and *Robocop* 2. The handful of other projects that he handled were either tv movies or shows. *Empire Strikes Back* would also introduce us to Yoda, an integral character to the franchise, and a testament to the power of practical effects. That little guy was literally just a hand puppet but god damn if you didn't buy into him, although still to this day, if I close my eyes when he's talking, all that I can picture is Fozzie Bear. Speaking of hand puppets, there's also a giant space worm thing the crew finds themselves in the mouth of, that I

36

guess is called an exogorth. The interesting thing about watching any of the *Star Wars* series is that if there's a character or creature that appears on screen for even 2 seconds, you can find an entire wealth of information online about them. For example, the space slug thing appears for this one shot of this one movie, and yet is listed as having around 20 to 30 mentions within various novels and ancillary releases. This film also gives us the live action debut of Boba Fett, because he had first appeared in an animated form in the *Star Wars Holiday Special*, although people tend to forget that one, or at least try to. After showing up in this one, people instantly fell in love, and launched a decades long mystery about whether or not his action figure actually had a firing rocket pack. And the answer is that it existed in a prototype form but was never released, so when you hear people talk about they personally knew someone that had one and choked to death, you can be confident that they're a lying sack of avocados. The budget on this one was just over $30 million, almost three times the price of the original, and was considered to be a gamble. This was back in an era where sequels were not guaranteed successes, and no one quite knew if the first film was lightning in a bottle. That proved to be unnecessary worrying though, since it went on to huge numbers, raking in just over $200 million, making it the highest grossing film of the year, practically double the take of the second highest. It didn't do quite as well as *Star Wars*, but it was still a massive win, and with multiple rereleases over time, its haul has increased even further and currently sits at half a billion dollars. In the '90s, around the time of the release of the prequels, it was sent back out with the others in the *Special Edition* versions, and contained a host of either new or altered scenes. The wampa, which was only glimpsed in the original cut, was given a full body reveal and other effects were cleaned up. Later editions contained further alterations, including swapping out the presentation of the Emperor and the voice acting of Fett. As the middle film of the trilogy, it's since become regarded as the best of them, with most considering it the best *Star Wars* related project ever. It's even the source of an oft-quoted sequence from *Clerks*, in which the film's "down ending" is credited for being the reason it is so well remembered.

My Rating - **4.5**. Look, I'm sure that I'll get some flack here for not giving this the full 5, but I'll admit that I'm not really a *Star Wars* guy. When I was younger, i was a bit more attracted to it all, but the Prequels possibly soured my enthusiasm for the universe. I suppose I was into the originals as much as any youngster at the time, but it just wasn't my main focus, and after *Return of the Jedi*, it fell out of my fandom entirely. That being said, there's no denying that this is a fantastic sci-fi action film, and when it comes to something like *Star Wars*, this is pretty much everything that you would want. It has thrilling battle sequences, great character moments, and moves the story forward in an unexpected way. And, yeah, much like Dante, i feel like the fact that it's not an optimistic film in which good clearly triumphs over evil works in its favor. It works as a story unto itself, but it also leaves things open enough to work as the middle portion of a trilogy.

Cultural Significance - **5.** Yeah, there's no way this isn't a 5 in terms of relevance. There's few films out there with the sort of cultural impact that the *Star Wars* series has, so it deserves as high of a ranking as it can get. And this episode in particular seems to have more recognition than others, and gave us the introduction of characters who would become some of the most known in the franchise with the little green guy and the bounty hunter. Plus, consider exactly how ingrained into the minds of the public that the phrase, "Luke, I am your father" has become, even if that's not the actual line.

Should You Watch It? Uh…you haven't? Really?

Sequel? Yes. Of course, this is the 2nd part of the original trilogy, but there's now been 7 films after this one, and then 2 side stories, as well as tv series, books, comics, video games, and every single other piece of merchandise that's humanly possible.

Remake? No.

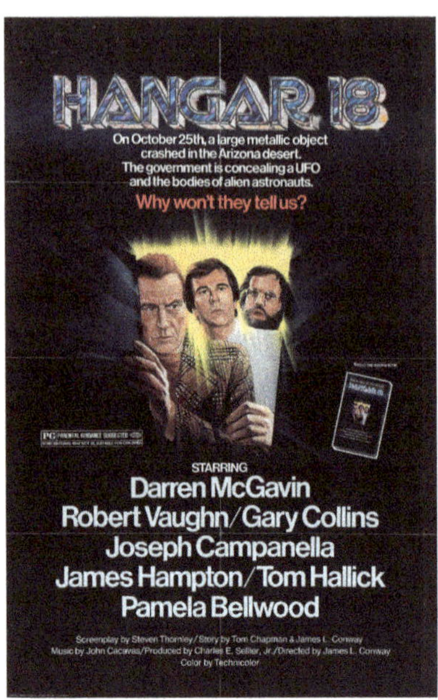

June 25th, '80
HANGAR 18

We're still in the realm of space ships on June 25th, when *Hangar 18* was released, predating the Megadeth song by about a decade. It's got Kolchak (Darren McGavin) working at NASA, while a space mission that features Teen Wolf's dad (James Hampton) sees a mysterious object collide with their satellite launch. It kills one of their men out there, and just like, pops his head off like a frozen Easter bunny. That object turns out to be some sort of space ship, which then lands in Arizona, and the Man from UNCLE (Robert Vaughn) shows up, and weirdly, he's played so many military guys. Just flipping through his roster of characters, it seems like every third one has some sort of rank in front of the name. It's kinda weird. The surviving astronauts are silenced upon landing, as the military decide that they need to cover the incident up. Because of this, the explosion and death are blamed on Lew and Steve, so they decide that they have no choice but to prove what really happened up there. Meanwhile, McGavin's Harry Forbes is leading up a group of scientists that are trying to study the alien ship and the mysteries within. This one was directed by James L.

Conway, who also directed the horror flick, *The Boogens*, as well as another sci-fi featured entitled *Earthbound*, but then shifted into directing TV shows, and is still very active in the industry. One of the weirder aspects of it is that the production company that handled it were mostly known for making documentaries, and when they marketed this one, they sort of teased that it was one as well. They pegged it as some sort of actual expose that would reveal the truth of UFOs instead of simply being a narrative film. The title, *Hangar 18*, comes from an actual place that is rumored to house the bodies of aliens from a UFO crash back in 1947, the Roswell crash. Although it's said that this film inspired the Megadeth song of the same name, it's more likely taken from the actual conspiracy theory than this movie. And another weird thing about this one is the ending, since it's…well…a bit of a downer. It's just sort of out of the blue depressing, and everyone dies. Everyone. And that's what played in the theaters. You left your screening with every single character that you met being blown up. There's even a news report that plays to let you know that they were all killed, in case you thought that the explosion was ambiguous. However, in 1983, the was aired on television as *Invasion Force*, and was given a new, upbeat ending. The explosion remains, but the news report is changed to state the cast survived, shielded by the ship, and its existence is revealed to the world. It seems to have a hefty price tag, considering the smaller scale of the film, at $11 million dollar and was a flop when released, earning back on $6 million.

41

My Rating - 2.5. This one starts off fairly promising, with the setup in outer space and that decapitation scene setting this off. But, just when it seems like it's getting you primed for some high adventure, it ends up settling back and kicking on the autopilot for the next hour. I truly don't understand the notion of promoting this as some sort of expose of the truth behind aliens, since it just comes off as a pretty standard tale. Sure, there's a government coverup involved, and it feels like it's trying to get at the "true story of Roswell," but it's presented in a similar fashion to any alien spacecraft tale, and ends up just feeling like something we've seen over and over again.

Cultural Significance - 2. This one gets a slight boost in terms of recognition, based on the fact that it does have a couple of names involved, even if they're of the "hey, I know that guy from something" variety. Plus, it did get enough of a reputation to earn it a spot on MST3K.

Should You Watch It? Maybe. As long as you're prepare for it to not exactly be super thrilling.

Sequel? No.

Remake? No.

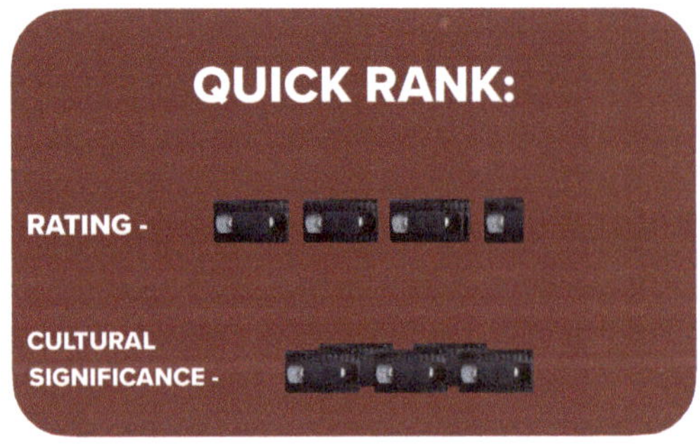

THE FINAL COUNTDOWN

Aug 1st, '80
THE FINAL COUNTDOWN

Going into August now, on the first of the month, we have a movie with a title that is virtually impossible to just say, you have to sing it, and it's *The Final Countdown*. Da da dun dun. Da da dun dun dun. It kicks off by giving you the villain of the

Spawn movie (Martin Sheen) and there's an extreme shock when you watch the opening credits and see the name, Lloyd Kaufman. He shows up there as an associate producer, and if you're not familiar with Lloyd, he's the co-founder of Troma, the company that gave you the cinematic gems of *Toxic Avenger* and *Class of Nuke 'Em High*. Before Troma took off, Lloyd was working random jobs on mainstream films, and this was one of them, and it's as far away from a Troma style production as you can get. It takes place on an aircraft carrier, the Nimitz, and Spartacus (Kirk Douglas) is here, for his second appearance in this volume. Unexpectedly, a strange storm pops up and engulfs the warship in a weird light and mist that looks like a typical '80s optical effect, but then subsides. When everything clears up, they've lost contact, and that's when you realize that he not only served as a producer on the film, but Kaufman appears in the film as a character. Not just that, but the character's name is Lloyd, and he's credited as Commander Kaufman. Waring Hudsucker (Charles Durning) shows up as a US Senator, and Mrs. Robinson's daughter is here as well (Katharine Ross), and by using radio broadcasts and reconnaissance photos, the crew realize that they have been transported in time to the day before the attack on Pearl Harbor in 1941. They're then faced with an ethical dilemma. With the knowledge of the attack and firepower on the carrier, they could alter history and turn the tide of the war, but should they? The director here is Don Taylor, who had been in the biz for decades by this point, and made *Escape From The Planet Of The Apes*, as well as the second *Omen* movie. And if

you were curious, yes, this IS where Europe got the name for their song, and magic …or excuse me… illusions would never be the same. But the production of this film was a disaster. Right before shooting, the production company were the victims of con artists, who suckered them out of a couple hundred thousand dollars, which reduced the overall budget of the film, and when they went over the scheduled shooting time, the costs increased, making everyone involved unhappy. In fact, it was the nonstop issues with the producers that caused Kaufman to leave the Hollywood system and strike out on his own. *The Final Countdown* did go on to be a minor hit, though not a big one, pulling in just under $17 million against a $12 million budget. Reviews on it were mixed, and Siskel and Ebert chose it as one of their "dogs of the year" awards.

My Rating - **3**. This one is like, half a good movie. There's some interesting concepts at work, and the time travel aspect is intriguing. The whole question of figuring out whether to change history is one that could be a fascinating subject to explore. Unfortunately, this one doesn't seem all that interested in doing that. It just raises these concepts that are ripe for exploring, and then ignores them and lets them sit in favor of shots of planes taking off. I wouldn't mind for someone to do another take on this and do a remake of sorts, but expand it and really get into the things that it shies away from. One thing I won't criticize is the actors. They all seem to be pretty invested in what they're doing here, and give it their all, creating the impression that they're in a far deeper and more serious film than what it ended up being. Even Lloyd.

Cultural Significance - **3.5.** This one gets a little boost since it's a fairly remembered film, even if it never made it to blockbuster status. Its heavy rotation on cable and network tv back in the day ensured that people saw it, and it features a heavy roster of stars to boost it up there. Including Lloyd.

Should You Watch It? Yeah. Just be prepared to spend more time thinking about the stuff that it DIDN'T explore more than what you actually see on screen.

Sequel? No.

Remake? No.

Aug 8th, '80
XANADU

Just a few days later, on August 8th, it was shown that *Xanadu* isn't just where the word "rosebud" was spoken. It starts with a shot of a man watching the sun rise in the morning, and that seems pretty innocuous, but I'll come back to that in a second. Next, we see one of the Warriors (Michael Beck), who doesn't exactly come

out and play, and instead rips up some art and throws it out the window, where I suppose that it wakes up a wall mural, who proceed to dance to ELO. One of them is Sandy (Olivia Newton John) and they dance all right. They boogie with some effects going on that conclusively prove that this is the '80s. This might just be halfway or so into the year 1980, but this one scene is the most '80s thing you're gonna see. The women of the mural are the 9 Sisters, the Greek muses, and they dance through Los Angeles, and here's where I circle back to that sunrise. Because as soon as you realize that this is set on the west coast, you realize that I guess it's some sort of world in which the sun rises in the west and sets in the east? Anyway, Beck's Sonny is an artist who works for a record company, reproducing album covers and hates it, as he sees it as a waste of his talents. He spots one of the girls from the wall on an album cover and goes in search of her. He just sees a model on the cover of a rock album and then goes walking around the city, hoping to run into her. Well, instead, he meets a man who should be singing in the rain (Gene Kelly), but come on, let's face it, there's no rain in LA. (I wrote that joke during the rainiest winter in Los Angeles in about 20 years.) Sonny finally just randomly spots his dream girl and follows her into an abandoned theater where she's roller skating, and they meet and start seeing each other. Now, when I say seeing each other, I mean having choreographed skate routines, and the story is really just a string of song and dance fantasy numbers. It does include a pretty awesome musical number by the Tubes,as Sonny and Danny decide to open a new

club called Xanadu which leads to more fantasy musical extravaganzas. There's even an animated sequence which has a weird story behind it, and it's that this bit wasn't originally supposed to be in the movie. It seems the studio had a mandate for the amount of songs that they wanted to be in the picture, so in order to meet that, they had to include this tune. However, the song didn't really fit in anywhere, so they just decided to make it an unconnected fantasy scenario. And this one was torn to shred when it came out. Critics absolutely hated it, and it was nominated for a ton of Razzies, and won one for Worst Director for Robert Greenwald. Although this was pretty early in his work, he was able to recover from it, and went on to a pretty long career, and is currently doing a string of political documentaries. Not only did critics denounce it, but audiences did too, since it barely made back its budget. It took in $23 million against a $20 million budget, but the soundtrack was another story. It went on to become a worldwide success, getting positive reviews from critics, and went double platinum, giving Newton John two more number one hits. All in all, it sold more than 2 million copies in the US and more than 5 million

worldwide, making it far more profitable than the film it was the soundtrack to. Although it failed to make a big impact in 1980, the movie has since taken on a cult status, even inspiring a stage musical, and has earned a spot in kitsch lover's hearts.

My Rating - 3. Look, I'd love to get caught up in the re-evaluation of this one, and embrace it's "so bad, it's good" badge. And there's definitely parts of this movie in which that definitely hits me and I'm lost in the absurdity of it all. I mean, this is a movie

about a Greek muse appearing and helping a young man open up a disco club. Unfortunately, when it comes right down it, it's kinda dull. There's just no story to it all, and it takes too long to get anywhere. By the time that they even decide that they're going to open up a club, the movie's more than half over. Plus, as much as Newton-John charms as the goddess, Kira, Michael Beck falls a little flat as the romantic lead, and isn't really that much fun to watch. There is a good amount of fun to be had here, though, and every moment that Gene Kelly is on screen is a delight.

Cultural Significance - **3.5**. This is a weird one to rate here, because it really comes down the question of where the significance lies. Is it in the movie, or the soundtrack? Clearly, the music is what set this one in the minds of people, and were it not for

the album, the film may have simply become forgotten. But, then again, if not for the film, then the soundtrack wouldn't even exist, so they have to go hand in hand. Ultimately though, it deserves a pretty solid rating here, since it's grown a huge following and stands as Kelly's final film.

Should You Watch It? Sure. Just strap on your skates beforehand.

Sequel? No.

Remake? Not really, although it's possible to consider the stage musical version one. Honestly kinda surprised that no one has tried redoing it.

49

Sept 8th '80
BATTLE BEYOND THE STARS

The first September release with an actual date came out on the 8th, and it's *Battle Beyond The Stars*, although Wikipedia says July 25th. The opening theme song of this one just

absolutely kicks ass, and it's because it was from a young James Horner, in one of his earliest works as he only did a couple of films came before this. One of those was *Humanoids From The Deep*, which I discussed in the horror version of the Project, but he also did the hilarious *Jaws* knockoff, *Up From The Depths*, back in 1979. The opening of the film gives us another sort of take on that whole, giant ship passing overhead thing that every sci-fi film from this time frame did. It's heading towards a small, peaceful planet, but it's not too peaceful because a very young Kathy Griffin lives there, in her very first screen credit ever. She's just an extra, though, and is on screen for approximately two seconds. That massive ship turns out to be helmed by Space Nancy's Dad (John Saxon again), and they invade the planet and start killing people willy nilly.

Bill Denbrough (Richard Thomas) lives there, with his sister Stephanie (Julia Duffy), and the evil Sador says that he'll return in 7 days to take control of their world, Akir. Shad then offers to take an ancient ship into space to find help, and it has an AI voice to guide him, and he looks for mercenaries who are willing to come fight with them. If you're unfamiliar with the basic story setup, it's essentially a space remake of the classic Japanese film, *The Seven Samurai*. That already had an American remake with *The Magnificent Seven*, and this follows that same basic plot, with a script by the Oscar winning John Sayles, who also wrote 1980's *Alligator*. It makes use of quite a few miniature models for the spaceships, and they look fantastic, and several of the models were made by a budding James Cameron, who ended up doing a lot of the fx work. Besides him, it was a star studded set, because Bill Paxton was there as well, doing carpentry work on the sets. Directing duties were handled by Jimmy Murakami, who had just done the added scenes for *Humanoids From The Deep* and both that and this movie were produced by Roger Corman. Murakami didn't do much in the way of features after this, instead working in TV and animation. On his journey, Shad ends up meeting with the beautiful Nanelia, cowboy Hannibal (George Peppard), and the lizard-like Cayman, who travels with two aliens called the Kelvin. There's also a group of telepathic clones called Nestor, and their spokesman is played by the recently departed Earl Boen, mostly known as that really dickish doctor from the *Terminator* films. Their little group is rounded out by "You're Next, Webster" (Robert Vaughn), Striba : Werewolf Bitch (Sybil Danning), who of course is mostly naked, and they all agree to help defend Akir from Sador. Budgeted at $2 million, this was the most expensive film that Corman had produced up until that point, with a large portion of that money going towards hiring Vaughn and Peppard. In the end, it did okay, but wasn't that huge of a success. The reviews were mixed, with many just calling it a *Star Wars* ripoff, but it was profitable, especially after international distribution and cable rights. All said and done, it earned back a respectable $11 million, more than five times what it cost to make. Since then, it's gone on to become a cult classic and has been cannibalized for use in about a dozen other Corman flicks. Horner's score, in particular, was repeated in no less than 10 other productions, including the teen sex comedy, *Screwballs*. Although there was never any sort of follow up on screen, there was a comic book series in 2010 that served as a prequel. It gave the backstory of Nell, the AI ship, and the adventures of her original owner.

My Rating - 4. I happen to love this one. Besides the fact that it's a fun retelling of the Kurosawa tale, and does justice to that story, it also manages to stand on its own. And if you're a fan of this sort of sci-fi, this is a cornucopia of cool creatures and ships. Each scene introduces some new character that's a different creative alien, and they're all clever and interesting. Even though the characters are based on their Japanese prototypes, it distinguishes them enough in their settings that they become unique. I do have to admit that this was actually the first version of the story I saw. I watched *Seven Samurai* and *The Magnificent Seven* much later in my life, so it's not like I was comparing this one to those when i was watching. That maybe tainted my view of it, but what can i say? I'm a sucker for it.

Cultural Significance - 3.5. I can't rank this too high here, since it's still a cult classic, instead of a known hit. However, you can't deny it's well remembered, thanks to cable runs. Beyond that, it can be seen as boosting the visibility of Cameron, paving the way for him to become an industry juggernaut, as well as establishing Horner's experience with space sagas. Add to that the collection of notable genre faces, and you've got a solid significance.

Should You Watch It? Absolutely.

Sequel? No. 

Remake? No.

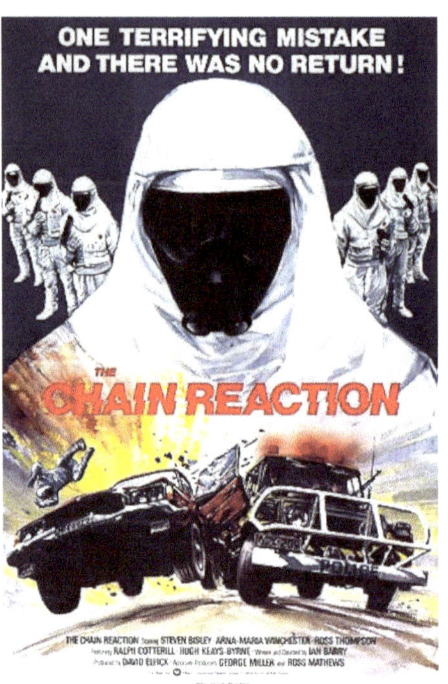

A few days later, on September 25th, on the other side of the world in Australia, we have the film, *The Chain Reaction.* It begins with an earthquake at a nuclear waste facility, two things that go great together, and when some of the toxic waste leaks, a dude does his impression of Jason in a Vancouver sewer. His bosses tell him that it was a fatal dose, and he tries to warn them that the leak will infect the groundwater nearby, a fact that they want to simply cover up, so he escapes to inform the public. Steve Bisley, from *Mad Max* is here, and he's not the only one. Mel Gibson sneaks in a minor cameo here and goes uncredited. In fact, quite a bit of the cast is actually from George Miller's flick and Miller was originally supposed to direct, but ended up pulling out, although he still worked on some of the chase sequences. Instead, it ended up being directed by Ian Barry, his first feature, and afterwards, he steadily continued to direct, but mostly in television. Heinrich, the escaped engineer, is saved by Bisley's mechanic character,

Larry, and his wife, but he only has three days to get the word out about the potential disaster while the company searches for him. Unfortunately, the accident has also given him memory issues, and has to struggle with remembering the very truth that he's trying to reveal. This ended up being a tough film to make on the limited budget they had. They requested $600,000, but were denied, instead being given $450,000. As they were shooting, though, they went over schedule, spent too much money, and ended up using $600k anyway. At this point, *The China Syndrome* had come out and was a huge hit, and panic about nuclear power was a popular theme, so the marketing on this leaned heavily into that. *The Chain Reaction* was originally intended as a dramatic film discussing the dangers of nuclear contamination, but during filming, became more action oriented and a touch sillier. It went on to become profitable, though not a major hit, in DVD reissues, they featured Mel Gibson's face taking up most of the cover, which is hilarious, because he's literally in 5 seconds of the movie. And keep in mind, that's not some sort of hyperbole, like, "oh, his role was so short, it felt like it was only 5 seconds." No, his actual screen time amounts to a total of an actual 5 seconds.

My Rating - 2.5. I'm a pretty big fan of the *Mad Max* movies. George Miller really did a great job with creating an entire world that felt both over the top and yet also weirdly real. Because of that, i was looking forward to this, even if he himself was not behind the camera calling the shots. Unfortunately, Barry is no Miller, and doesn't quite handle the action as deftly. There's some nice character work here and there, but the story itself just limps along, with no clear direction, and only really perks up when the car stuff happens. Not coincidentally, it appears as if most of the chase scenes were actually handled by Miller, and you can tell. They have a certain sure-handed feeling that you're not getting throughout the rest of the piece.

Cultural Significance - 2. Even though it does have a couple of big players involved, it's still a little obscure. So much that they had to put a guy that's in the movie for 5 second on the cover art in order to sell it.

Should You Watch It? Maybe? If you're a diehard fan of the *Mad Max* universe, this may have a sort of curiosity for you, but otherwise, there's not a whole lot that you're missing.

Sequel? No.

Remake? No.

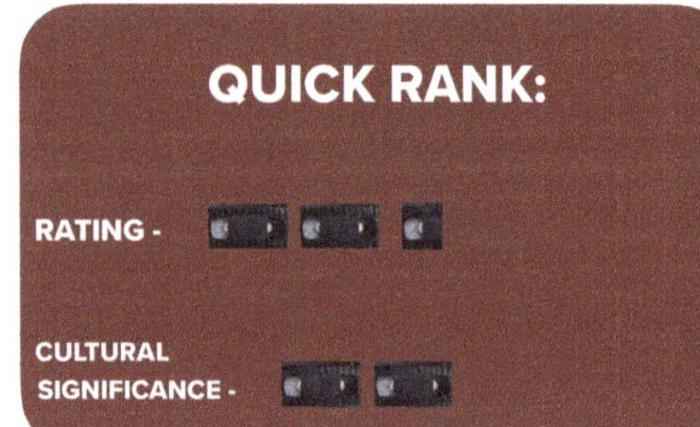

56

Imaged by Heritage Auctions, HA.com

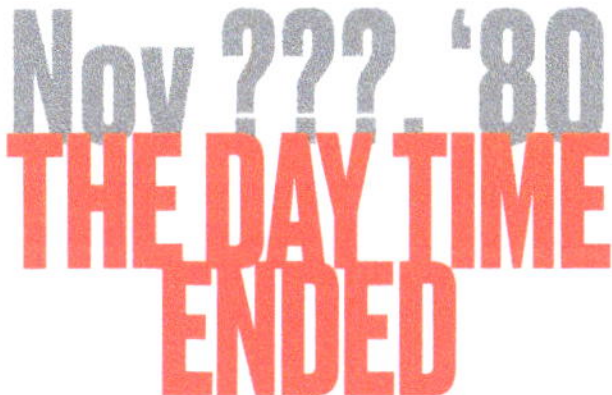

Here's a weird one that doesn't have a confirmed date, but it did come out in November and it's *The Day Time Ended*. It begins with classic cowboy actor Jim Davis (not the Garfield guy) and his family, including Chris Mitchum, son of Robert Mitchum, who is not James, who is a different Mitchum son that was featured previously in the horror version of the book in the entry for *Monstroid*. His fam is moving out to the desert, and grandson Steve is with them, played by Scott Kolden, who is one of those '80s actors who looks like he could be 14 years old, but could also easily be 32. A weird object materializes on their new property that looks like one of the pylons from *Land of the Lost*, and little granddaughter Jenny starts seeing odd things around the house, including a series of strange lights in the sky. This one was directed by John Bud Cardos, who is perhaps most known for doing *Kingdom of the Spiders*, and it was produced by Charles Band. This was before Band was the head of Full Moon, and even prior to starting Empire Pictures, but you could see the seeds starting to bloom here. His son Richard was on hand to do the music, and Ted Nicolau did the editing, both of whom would go on to become heavily involved in films for both companies. Another longtime Band collaborator, David Allen, is also on board to provide some cool stop motion creature effects. Pretty soon, there's little alien ships chasing them, giant monsters battling outside, and it starts to feel more like an FX reel than it does an actual movie. The family just end up coming up against challenge after challenge, although none of them seem to connect with each other, and it feels like an elaborate fever dream that attempts to be *Close Encounters of the Third Kind*, but also kinda doesn't? There's really no box office information on the film, although it was pretty poorly reviewed, with critics citing its aimlessness and pointing out the flaws in the low budget effects.

My Rating - 2. If you're sitting down and intending to watch a movie, then you're really not going to be happy here. There's really not much story, character development, arcs, or anything. It's a little bit enjoyable to have on and see an assortment of different unrelated creature effects popping onto the screen, though. Sadly, a lot of it looks a bit dated, although it doesn't matter too much when it has that classic stop motion charm to it. If you're a big fan of classic cheap fx, then you'll do worse than to watch this, but a lot of it plays better with the shadows of a couple of robots in the corner.

Cultural Significance = 1.5. There's really nothing here that stands out or is memorable in terms of the actual movie itself. It doesn't do anything to really stand out, since the only thing that's really of note in the film is the special effects, and a lot of them use techniques that were pretty standard in this era. It gets the extra .5 for presence of the Bands behind the scenes, and Allen's miniature contributions.

Should You Watch It? This one is pretty skippable, although I'd probably recommend watching the MST3K version for some laughs.

Sequel? No.

Remake? No.

QUICK RANK:

RATING -

CULTURAL SIGNIFICANCE -

Nov 21st, '80
THE APPLE

Here's one with a fixed date in November, and we get a weird experience called *The Apple*, and if you're watching these films in order, you might get a bit of Deja vu. Within the first couple of minutes, you'll start to feel like you've accidentally turned on *Xanadu* again. It starts off with a futuristic society full of disco folk, and then

introduces the evil Devil…I mean, Mr. Boogalow (Vladek Sheybal), who you may remember from the Bond film, *From Russia With Love*, as the evil Kronsteen. It's set in the distant future of 1994, and it's a big song competition, eerily prophetic of shows like *American Idol*. In a world obsessed with big pop tunes, new contestants Adam and Eve…I mean, Bibi (Catherine Mary Stewart) and Alphie (George Gilmour) come strolling out and play a simple love song that people go nuts for. Upset that the audience loves an act that he has no control over, Boogalow rigs the contest to his favor. Afterwards, he invites the duo to his place for a party where they start to tempt Bibi over to the dark side, but Alphie resists. And if you haven't gotten it by now, this is a biblical parable in a sci-fi musical form, and it would have been even more obvious if they have kept the original opening scene. In it, there was a god character seen creating the heavens and making Alphie, the first man, and sending him to Bibi. *The Apple* was both written and directed by Menaham Golan, the man behind Cannon films, and he's responsible for a laundry list of wild genre flicks. Earlier this year, Cannon had been responsible for *The Godsend* and *Schizoid*, but this was different. Golan made it to cash in on the disco craze, and he was so convinced it was going to be a hit that he increased the budget from $4 million to $10 million. A massive bible story set in a disco future with people forced to wear a sticker from a record label on their body or be forced to pay a fine, and a film in which the main hero walks up behind his landlady and gropes her. As stated, George Gilmour played that hero, and for whatever reason, this was his final film. His first film, as well. In fact, this is his only credit in the industry whatsoever. And that might be because when this first screened, it was a disaster. At a premiere in Montreal,

the studio made souvenir soundtrack records to give out, but during the screening, the audience began to throw them at the screen. Golan was so distraught by this reaction that he considered throwing himself off a hotel balcony. The only reason he did not was because his business partner returned to the room. *The Apple* was lambasted by the press and viewers, and was referred to as not only the worst movie of the year, but one of the worst of all time. The reaction over time has been interesting, with some embracing camp aspects of it, and others continuing to call it out as an overstuffed turkey. Some analyses of have pegged it as overly Christian, showing "evil" and "satanic" aspects of society to be more flamboyant. It's been called obviously homophobic and regressive, with Alphie's mission to lure Bibi away from what's being called a decadent lifestyle, and restore her to a more traditional role.

My Rating - 3. This one is pretty bad, sure. It's ridiculous, and such a misunderstanding of what general audiences were looking for that it's easy to see why it failed. It has cult success written all over it. Perhaps over time, the best cult films are the ones that failed at what they were trying to do, and inadvertently succeeded at doing something else, and this falls under that category. Most of the appreciation for this comes from a "this is so bad it's good" standpoint, as opposed to it being a misunderstood masterpiece. And I'm on board with that. But the primary reason I won't rate this one higher is the sheer fact that it's a musical without any good songs. As silly as Xanadu was, there was no way to walk away from it without humming or singing those main tracks, but here, you'll be hard pressed to remember anything about them.

Cultural Significance - 2. This gets some extra points for a cult following, but it's still under the radar, even for the niche market. Most of its notoriety is due to it being called a terrible movie, as opposed to a fun one. Add the fact that most of the performers in the film didn't achieve much success later, with the except of Stewart, and the most recognizable name involved being Golan himself.

Should You Watch It? If you like ridiculous, over the top, sci-fi musicals, then yes. Like, if you watched *Xanadu*, and said, "i want more of this, but even dumber," then this is the movie for you.

Sequel? No.

Remake? No.

QUICK RANK:

RATING -

CULTURAL SIGNIFICANCE -

Dec 4th, '80
SUPERMAN 2

This next entry may not really belong here, because it's *Superman 2*. Now, you may be reading this, saying "hey, wait. Didn't *Superman* 2 come out in the summer of 1981?" And yes, you're right. It did. But it played internationally all through the month of December in 1980, starting on the 4th in Australia. It played France and Norway on the 9th, Spain on the 11th, Italy on the 23rd, and Argentina and Brazil on Christmas Day. This was a pre-internet world in which people overseas couldn't spoil the entire movie online, and a film could be out in other countries for 6 months before their domestic release. Now, the behind the scenes of this movie is way, way too complicated for me to get into, as it could probably be an entire book unto itself, and I believe that there are several books doing exactly that, so I'll just be doing the short version here. Parts of this were shot at the same time as the first one, *Superman: The Movie*, but director Richard Donner was infamously fired with about 75% of complete. It seems that after the first film came out and before they started production on the rest of the sequel, Donner said unkind words about the Salkinds, the producers, and they gave him his notice. They then brought in Richard Lester, mostly known for more humorous action flicks like *The Three Musketeers*, and he revamped the script and shot the rest of the footage, as well as doing reshoots to reshape the film. There was a two year gap in between the scenes Donner shot and the new stuff, so you can see inconsistencies with the actors' looks. For instance, in the earlier footage, Christopher Reeve is less muscle bound, as he continued to bulk up for the

second film. The plot involves the accidental release of three Kryptonian villains from their prison in the Phantom Zone, who make their way to Earth and challenge the Man of Steel with powers that rival his own. Now, I mentioned this came out in December overseas, and this was because Warner Brothers made a unique decision to release the film worldwide in each country's peak film going season. At this point, the summer season had become the best time for blockbusters in America and Canada, they waited until June of '81, but in Australia, and the majority of Europe, they went with this December release, as those countries had massive theater attendance during the Christmas season. That gamble paid off, as the movie was massively successful, and it became the top grossing film of 1981. Critics dug it too, with Roger Ebert giving it 4 out of

4 stars. And you know, it's not exclusive to this movie, since it's a factor in the first one as well, but attention needs to be drawn to Reeve's portrayal of Clark Kent. I know it's been said before, but it bears repeating. The concept of Superman's disguise being a pair of glasses is ludicrous when you think about it, but when he's playing Kent, his entire body language changes. His demeanor, appearance…everything. He turns into another character, and I believe that people wouldn't be able to tell the difference. Since its release, it's only increased its status, with some liking it more than original, due to having an actual physical challenge with Zod and his crew. And,

oh yeah, about that. In case you were wondering why Superman seemed so blasé about what is now 3 completely powerless human opponents falling to their deaths in his Fortress of Solitude, you can rest easy. I know it's not exactly canon, since it's a deleted scene, but there's a moment that takes place afterwards showing the trio being arrested, proving that they're still alive, and I guess going to jail. Kind of brings into question exactly who are arresting them. Supes' hideout is in the Arctic Circle, and the scene takes place very shortly after their big fight, so what jurisdiction is that exactly? And how did they get there so fast? With police cars? I guess I can see why that scene was deleted. Does that mean that they really did die? I guess only Clark and Lois can answer that one.

My Rating - 4.5. This is one of my favorite superhero flicks of all time. I think that I like the original a touch more, but there's not much off here. From a script level, it's one of the most rounded you're getting. It gives characterization to our heroic characters, but also finds time to make our villains interesting. And I'm not just talking about Zod, Ursa, and Non. It manages to throw in Lex Luthor in there, too, and still give him enough screen time so he doesn't feel tacked on. That being said, i can't give this one a full 5, since Lester felt the need to shoehorn in dopey comic relief. Some of slapstick justs fall flat and take it down a peg. The Donner cut of the film, released over 40 years later, rectifies a bit of that, but it has its own issues.

Cultural Significance - 4.5. The significance of this is the same, since it's often considered the gold standard for superhero movies. Once again, though, I have to hold it back from the full 5 as it's a sequel, instead of the original item, lending a bit of its notoriety towards that one existing.

Should You Watch It? Yes. If you say you don't want to...would you care to step outside?

Sequel? Yes. This version of the series had two more entries, with a belated partial sequel coming decades later with Superman Returns. The franchise was then rebooted with Man of Steel into the DCEU, and will soon be rebooted again, in a film with James Gunn directing.

Remake? No, although certain elements of this one would be repeated in Man of Steel.

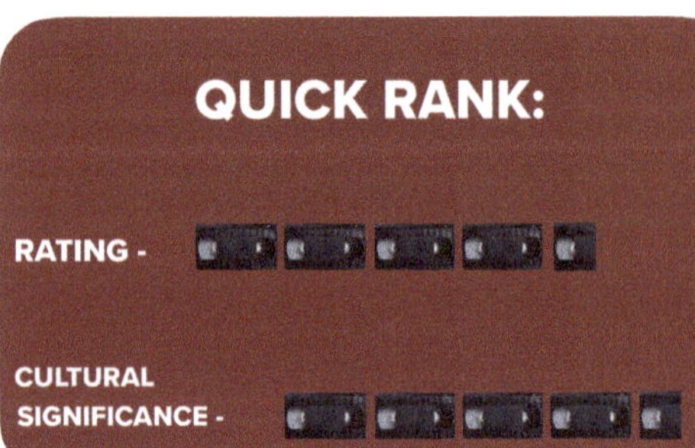

QUICK RANK:

RATING -

CULTURAL SIGNIFICANCE -

Dec 5th, '80
FLASH GORDON

Superman 2 may not have been released in the US by this point, but that doesn't really matter when that month also produced one of

the wonders of the film world. Yes, one of the greatest additions to the lexicon of cinema occurred with the arrival of *Flash Gordon*. Right here is where you imagine lofty voices all singing AHH AHHHHH. We're introduced to football star, Flash Freaking Gordon (Sam Jones), who is so damn cool that he wears a t-shirt with his own name emblazoned on the front of it. There's a quick flash of Robbie Coltrane here, as a guy helping Flash onto an airplane, and after about 2 seconds, he's gone. If you're not familiar, this is an adaptation of a classic comic strip from the '30s, and it had previously been brought to life with several film serials with Buster Crabbe, but at this point, 40 years had passed since the last of those.

There's a mysterious, evil guy on another planet who is sending disasters to earth, like giant hail balls, which catches the attention of semi mad scientist, Dr. Hans Zarkoff (Topol). He ends up recruiting Flash against his will, along with the lovely Dale Arden (Melody Anderson) to go up in a rocket to find the source of the attacks. The trio land on the planet Mongo, where they meet the awesome Prince Vultan of the hawk people, played by the amazing Brian Blessed, who is clearly having a blast. There's also Prince Barin, or Neville Sinclair (Timothy Dalton), and they find Mongo's ruler, Brewmeister Smith (Max Von Sydow) and his lackey Klytus (Peter Wyngarde), one of the only characters created for the film. And everything over the top. The colors, costumes, performances…everything. It has, hands down, one of the greatest soundtracks in history, all by Queen, which makes every scene more impactful, and less… well…silly.

Like, there's a scene where Flash fights the royal guard by playing football against them, using an ornate egg as a ball. It's absurd, with Dale acting as a cheerleader to root him on, but the very second that "Football Fight" kicks in, the moment is sold. The shoot was extremely troubled, and didn't have a finished script while filming. Mike Hodges, the director, called it the first improvised $27 million film. Hodges had previously done *Get Carter,* and *The Omen 2*, and this was a bigger project than he had previously been involved. There were also issues with the star, Sam Jones, since after principal photography, he tried to renegotiate with producer, Dino De Laurentiis, to get more money. Of course, this didn't go over well, and they didn't call him in to do post production work. They called his bluff and and dubbed nearly all of Jones' dialogue with another actor. His actions earned him a reputation of being difficult to deal with, and prevented him from getting cast in later projects. In the film, you can spot small roles for Riff Raff (Richard O'Brien), Charles Grady (John Osborne), Deep Roy, and Andy Warhol girl, Viva. Plus, if you're a Time Bandits fan, the palace scene on Mongo features almost the entire little person cast of that film, along with Kenny Baker. It's got one of my favorite action sequences with the assault on War Rocket Ajax, and it's just non-stop joy. Critics thought so too, and gave it nice reviews, but audiences weren't as sold. It's performance at the theaters was so-so and wasn't nearly the hit they were hoping for. The studio was expecting *Star Wars* numbers, and it didn't come anywhere near that, although still made a profit.

Costing

around $20 million, it made around $27 million in the US, and also did well in the UK, but the rest of its worldwide take was inconsequential. Those numbers, in combination with the soured relationship with Jones, meant that a sequel wasn't in the cards, even though they clearly teased one in the ending shot. By the way, that hand belonged to Klytus, who seemed to die in the film, but they intended to bring him back. Over time, though, the film's appeal has only increased, becoming a huge success, and is often cited as a major influence of stylistic directors like Edgar Wright.

My Rating - **5**. Sorry, not sorry. This is one of my favorite films of all time. I know that it's cheesy and campy, but that was intentional. There was a conscious decision to ape a comic style here, and it's one of the rare times that I feel like a movie aimed for that aesthetic and managed to succeed. But there's two reasons why this will always be at the top for me. I know that one of them is sheer nostalgia, since I loved this movie when i was younger and wanted to be Flash Gordon. Sure, i never went out and bought a shirt with my name on the front, but he was the sort of hero that I admired. But, the second, and the most important, is that soundtrack. Queen absolutely killed it here, and it's this pitch perfect mixture of a score and songs. Plus, after all, he saved every one of us.

Cultural Significance - **4**. This is far up on the roster, because it's instantly recognizable. It's widely known and has a ton of known actors, had a huge influence on other sci-fi, and adapted a classic character. The only reason it doesn't get higher is because of that initial near miss at the box office.

Should You Watch It? Yes. And then buy the soundtrack. And then be happy.

Sequel? Sadly, no.

Remake?
Surprisingly no. Not only have there been no remakes of this film, but there really haven't been any further progress with bring the character to the screen at all. There's been some animated series, as well as some doomed attempts at a feature relaunch, but nothing has materialized as of yet.

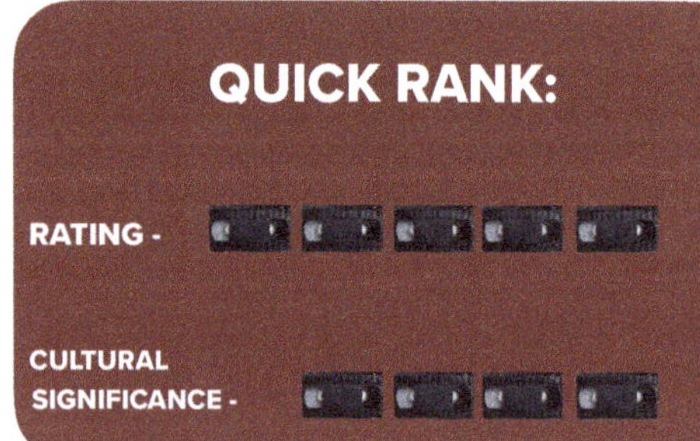

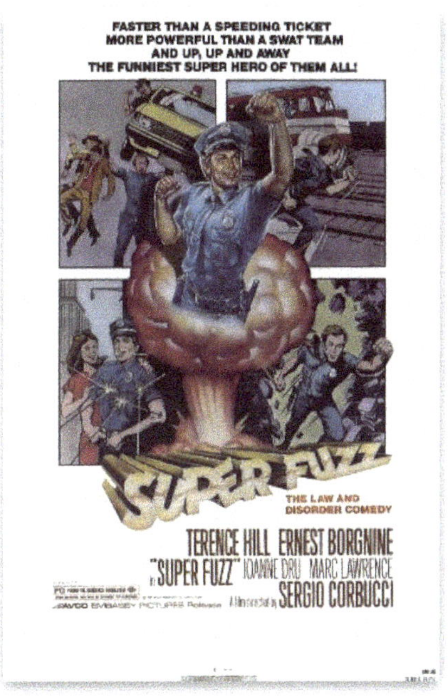

Dec 7th, '80
SUPER FUZZ

2 days later, on December 7th in Italy, another cult classic was born with *Super Snooper*, although it would be released in the US in 1981 as *Super Fuzz*, and anyone with HBO in the '80s has seen this around 1000 times. Like *Flash Gordon*, it also has an amazing theme song, and much like that one, it primarily consists of repeating the characters

name over and over again. There's an opening newscast that tells us about a cop named Dave who killed his partner, but they've been unable to execute him. On his long walk, he flashes back to his story, and Dave Speed is played by Terrance Hill, a pretty popular comic actor in Italy in the '70s who was know for westerns and cop movies. So, I've never really been clear about what happens in the early part of the film, because they're doing some sort of experimental rocket test, and i assume that it's part of their plan to to detonate it. However, Dave is inadvertently in the area, and is confronted by a crocodile, and in an effort to scare it off, shoots his gun into the air. So, I'm not sure if they're saying that he's responsible for the explosion, or if it's just a coincidence. If it's the former, then that gun has one hell of a range, or else that rocket was flying awful low. After the explosion, Dave is presumed dead, but then he just shows back up and greets his partner, Ted

Denslow (Ernest Borgnine), and seems to have enhanced abilities like telekinesis, precognition, and when he's tossed out of a high rise window, the ability to transform into a dummy and then back again. But then he also has slightly super speed, super strength, and the ability to make an entire stadium of people disappear. It's unclear if he teleports them somewhere, or just makes them stop existing momentarily. No one reacts to being displaced and then returned to where they once were, so I guess he blinked them out of being for a moment, which is kind of terrifying. He can mass disintegrate thousands, and then restore them in perfect form, which is a fairly godlike ability. And this was the work of Sergio Corbucci, a prolific Italian director and the guy who made the original *Django* movie. You know, the one that Quentin Tarantino liked the title of so much that he just stole it? And if you had

cable in the '80s, this is another that there was no escape from. If you turned on your TV and flipped enough stations, you'd eventually find Super Fuzz. Although it was an Italian production, they made it with American distribution in mind, which is why they filmed in Florida. Dave has an weakness in that he loses his power if he sees the color red, which is a little broad. I mean, there's red everywhere. How much does there have to be? How pure does it have to be? What is the threshold between red, and say, pink? And it's a weird film. It's a superhero story where he never puts on any sort of costume, and spends most of the time in either a police uniform or street clothes. There's no clear record of just how big of a release it was or how well it did at the box office, but it's obvious that it made a good deal of money by selling off the cable rights, and has certainly gone on to become a bit of a cult sensation.

My Rating - 3.5. I want to give this a 4, based entirely on nostalgia, but unlike *Flash Gordon,* which still gives me the same charge when I watch it today, this has lost its luster. I still think it's a ton of fun, and an enjoyable watch, but just don't think it holds up as well. It's just such a weird film that it's hard to get mad at it, but it never really seems to have a point. There's a sort of villain in the movie, but it's not really clear what his whole goal is, except to just be a criminal. So, the plot just kind of wanders around, from wacky set piece to wacky set piece, as Dave tries to figure out his powers. But then, suddenly, in the final fifteen minutes, they decide to have a finale so everything just sort of happens. And Hill's performance as Dave is just hilariously stifled. He was well known for his comic roles, but looking back, I'm not really sure why. He has about 2 facial expressions. Happy and shocked.

Cultural Significance - 2.5. Much like I want to rate my personal ranking of this one a touch higher, I want to give this a 3 as well. But it was really only relevant and known for a very specific period of time, and never gained any significant steam beyond that. Plus, it's not like it really impacted the genre, although it did introduce some interesting concepts regarding superpowers, but then never explored any of them.

Should You Watch It? Sure. Enjoy the silliness, and then try to get that theme song out of your head.

Sequel? No.

Remake? No.

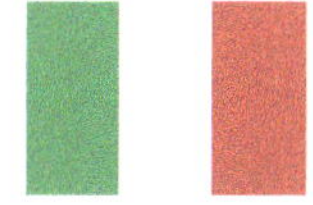

??? THE RETURN

Our final entry for 1980 doesn't have a confirmed release date as it's only known to have a limited run in 1980, and it's *The Return*. This has an alien ship arriving in a small town, entrancing a young girl and boy. One of those evil Lectroids is here (Vincent Schiavelli) and he's abducted. It then jumps to 25 years later, and Maddie Hayes (Cybill Shepherd) shows up, with her father

Steve Martin (Raymond Burr). She's a scientist who discovers an anomaly in Little Creek, a small town where Air Wolf (Jan-Michael Vincent) is a police officer. And I feel like enough time has passed that I can say Jan Michael Vincent without people quoting *Rick and Morty* one thousand times at me. He pulls over a couple of speeders and when they won't get out of their car, he shoots their radio. This is the '80s, and this was the expected behavior of the "rogue cop." It's weird that there was this point in time that viewers would think this was a good and acceptable thing to happen. Bela Lugosi (Martin Landau) is on hand, and when there's a series of cattle mutilations, the old miner from the intro is there, but hasn't aged. It's soon revealed that Officer Wayne and scientist Jennifer were those kids from the opening, and UFO shenanigans and fate have brought them together. This one was directed by Greydon Clark, who had also directed *Without Warning*, which is covered in the horror book. By all reports, filming was rough, as Vincent was having issues with alcoholism and would interfere with their scheduling. He didn't show up one day, and they had to recover by convincing Shepard and Landau to come to set on their days off. It's clear they were aiming for a *Close Encounters* vibe, but it never took off and didn't get the theatrical run *Without Warning* achieved, only reaching a wider audience a few years later on TV runs and video.

My Rating - **2**. I find it hard to believe this was intended for theatrical release when it feels like a TV movie. It fails to give off the vibes that *Without Warning* was able to, which was also done on a low budget. And I know he has the backing of internet meme lords, but I've never been a Vincent fan. The fact that he was struggling is blatantly obvious, given his sleepwalking through this film. Thankfully, Landau

and Schiavelli pick up his slack, and appear to be having a good time, and are possibly the best reason to check this one out.

Cultural Significance - **2**. I'm a touch hesitant to give this one a two, as opposed to a 1.5 or something, but it's hard to argue with the cast in terms of notoriety. With Clark behind the scenes, and the involvement of Landau, Schiavelli, Vincent, Shepard, and Burr, there's enough to give it a touch more relevance, even if it is a bit forgotten.

Should You Watch It? You can skip this one pretty easily.

Sequel? No.

Remake? No.

Jan 5th, '81
THE HITCHHIKER'S GUIDE TO THE GALAXY

Ok. I know that I'm sort of breaking my own rules here because this isn't a movie, and isn't even a TV movie, but on January 5th, 1981, in the UK, *The Hitchhiker's Guide To The Galaxy* debuted as a TV miniseries. I don't normally cover series, and the Project is mainly about movies, but there's no way that i'm not going to talk about an adaptation of one of the greatest books of all time. We start off by meeting Arthur Dent, average human, who is dealing with the fact that his house is about to be destroyed. I feel like I should make a comment about how it's not a house, it's a home, but only the 10 people who played the old text game of *Hitchhiker's* would get it. His good friend Ford Prefect is not human, but Arthur doesn't know that. He tells him, but also informs him that the earth is about to be destroyed by an alien fleet. Luckily, he has a means to escape onto the ship, while the planet is detonated below them. Now, it's pretty ballsy to start off your series with the planet literally being obliterated, but the pair then head out on a series of adventures, eventually meeting up with the stolen ship, The Heart of Gold, which travels through the use of an improbability drive. Onboard is Marvin the paranoid Android, an old flame of Arthur's named Trillion, and the President of the galaxy, Zaphod Beeblebrox. And if you're not familiar with this, it's based on a book by the great Douglas Adams, and is possibly one of the most influential works of science fiction and comedy out there. It actually didn't begin as a book. It started as a radio play for BBC radio back in 1978, and spun into different forms of media from there. The '81 series marked the first live action version of the story, and used a number of actors from the radio show. It would end up winning a number of awards and run for 6 episodes, following our crew to the lost planet of Magrathea, visiting the Restaurant at the End of the Universe, and ending up on prehistoric earth. Along the way, they discover the secret to life, the universe, and well…everything. Adams himself would write the scripts for the show, and weirdly, there's no director credited, although all episode were handled by Alan J.W. Bell, who did quite a bit of TV work, but was mainly devoted to a show called *Last of the Summer Wine* and he did 250 episodes of it. And with how much I enjoy this story, and even this particular version of it, I feel like I should have so much more to say about it, but I wrote this on a Thursday, and I never could get the hang of those.

My Rating - **4.5**. It's hard for me to put into words what this story means to me. I'm impacted by every form of it: the book, the radio show, the feature film, and this miniseries, which was actually my very first exposure to it all. Because of it, I've tried to find a way to work the number 42 into practically everything. And this version hits all the right notes, even if some of the effects are painfully dated. Thankfully, the comedy isn't, and the line readings here are what I hear in my head when I reread the book. If you're unfamiliar with this whole story, I'm not completely sure that this miniseries is the best introduction to it because you might be distracted by the retro aspect of things, but it's also not a terrible way to experience it, since it's a magical take on a magical tale.

Cultural Significance - **3**. I've dropped this a touch from my initial take in the video version of things, but it's still the first shot at putting this on screen and won a bunch of awards, but it's just not the most well known version of it and didn't impact things overseas.

Should You Watch It? Yeah, you hoopy frood!

Sequel? No. Plans for a second series fell apart after budget disputes.

Remake? Yes. Although it can be argued that the 2005 film is less a remake of this and is simply another take on the source book.

Jan 30th, '81
THE INCREDIBLE SHRINKING WOMAN

Our next entry is from January 30th and it's *The Incredible Shrinking Woman*, directed by Joel Schumacher, his first theatrical film. It gives us Edwina Cutwater (Lily Tomlin) as a typical suburban mom, and Lily Tomlin actually plays several roles in the film, selling herself beauty products, and her husband is Beethoven's dad (Charles Grodin). He works for an ad agency and is always bringing home new products for her to test out, and his boss is the Mayor of Otisburg (Ned Beatty), and Castor Oyl (Donovan Scott) pops in a for a second, and they soon notice that Pat has begun to get shorter. She goes for all sorts of tests with her doctor being an Illinois Nazi (Henry Gibson), and he explains that the mixture of all the chemicals in her house have caused her to begin shrinking. Pretty soon she's smaller than her kids, and a national news story sensation, until they realize they need to cover up what happened to her. This one started out as a John Landis film with a much bigger budget, but when Universal decided that they wanted to scale it back and took it from a 30 million dollar picture to a 10 million dollar one, he dropped a helicopter on someone, or I mean, dropped out of the film, and Schumacher stepped in. A little later on in the picture, Daniel Clamp (John Glover) shows up as a villain, and the story is basically a parody of commercialism and the inundation of advertising and products. It was written by Jane Wagner, who is a regular collaborator with Tomlin, as the two are married and have been together since the 70's. There's also the inclusion of one of my personal favorites, Mark Blankfield, and a gorilla named Sydney, and the suit was made by the legendary Rick Baker, shortly before he won an Oscar for *American Werewolf*, and he actually plays Sydney. That's Baker inside the suit. And if you squint really really hard you can catch Julie Brown in one of her earliest roles. If you blink you'll miss it, but she on the TV as a commercial spokesperson. The role was due to Tomlin seeing Brown perform and thinking she was great, but most of the scenes they shot with her were cut out. However, Brown is still thankful for the role, since it earned her a SAG card. When this one came out it was pretty negatively reviewed, although it was fairly successful, earning just over $20 million, making back double its budget, which isn't really a huge hit, but is still a nice profit.

80

My Rating - 3.5. This is another one that I probably watched several hundred times during those golden days of HBO. However, it's one that I didn't revisit and in watching it for this entry, it had been a solid couple of decades since I'd seen it. And it holds up pretty well. The commentary on corporate product saturation is even more poignant today and the impact that consumerism affects our everyday health still rings true. Tomlin steals the show and she didn't have a large amount of comic lead roles where she was front and center as opposed to being a part of an ensemble, so it's great to see her really be able to shine. I do wish that it was more consistent overall, though, since some of the tone and comic bits don't exactly mesh, and the plot elements that lead up to the finale are introduced a little too late, but it doesn't hold it back from being a ton of fun.

Cultural Significance - 3. This gets a bit of extra oomph for being a quasi remake of a sci-fi classic, as well as featuring a whole slew of known names. Beyond that, it was Schumacher's first film and contained top notch work by Baker.

Should You Watch It? Yes. Make a little time for it.

Sequel? No.

Remake? No.

QUICK RANK:

RATING -

CULTURAL SIGNIFICANCE -

Jan 30th, '81
EARTHBOUND

On that same day, January 30th, there was a low budget release called *Earthbound*, which starts off with Burl Ives, and there's just no possible way to hear this guy's voice without thinking of Christmas time. There's a kid named Tommy, and his parents have died, so he's now living with his grandfather, and a mysterious object enters Earth's atmosphere. Stuart Pankin is here for everyone who used to watch *Not Necessarily The News*, and a spacecraft appears before a small town, causing chaos. Rumors are spread that the major cities have already been destroyed, but the aliens are actually a very human looking family that seem to have some sort of powers and also have a chimp with them that is meant to be an alien that they found on their travels around the galaxies. Ned and Tommy take them in while the military is on the hunt, and this one was directed by James I. Conway, who directed 1980's *Hangar 18* which was also about humans encountering a ufo, but a dramatically different take than this. We'll also see him in the horror version of the Project with *The Boogens*, but then he pretty much switched entirely to directing TV series. And in fact, that's how this one started. It was meant as a pilot for a TV show that would follow this space family and their adventures on earth, but it was turned down by every network, so it was then slightly re-edited and then released as a movie theatrically. It was promoted as "a very spacey comedy," although the humor really isn't at the forefront. It's more of a family film than anything, and it's got a small part for a guy that I mostly know from *Surf 2* and *Under The Rainbow* (Peter Isacksen). And yeah, it's pretty easy to see how it was passed on for a series, as it didn't really make a dent at the box office either and has sort of fallen into obscurity.

My Rating - 1. Holy cow is this one dull. Like, extremely dull. There's just so little happening and the things that do happen just aren't interesting. Plus, everything about this one reeks of TV movie of the week, except even cheaper. Hell, the only thing in this one that consistently got my attention was the monkey, and even that guy seemed embarrassed to be associated with what was going on.

Cultural Significance - 1. This is almost entirely forgotten. It's one that I hadn't even heard of or seen the box art for before tracking it down, and after watching it, it's clear why. No one wanted this on their TV screens back then, and they sure don't want it now either.

Should You Watch It? Hard pass.

Sequel? No.

Remake? No.

Apr 10th, '81
THE LAST CHASE

Then, on April 10th, we got the action sci-fi flick, *The Last Chase*, which was a partially Canadian production. We have a 6 million dollar man (Lee Majors), who has a new, high-tech car, but gas is a commodity, and a good portion of humanity has been wiped out by a strange plague, including hart's family. There's no more cars, so everyone has to either walk or ride bikes, which sounds kind of horrifying, but also…kinda awesome. Oh, but it's also a totalitarian dictatorship, and that parts really not kinda awesome at all. Hart is a spokesman for the mass transit system, but when he finds out about a hidden territory called free California that has seceded from the US, he decides to try to make it there. Rudy from *Meatballs* is here (Chris Makepeace), and he and Hart are forced to go on the run in Hart's revamped Porsche. The Penguin (Burgess Meredith) is in this one too, as a retired Air Force pilot that they bring in to track down and kill Hart, and this one was directed by Martin Burke, who didn't do a whole lot, but he did write the comedy classic, *Top Secret*. At the time, there was a hope with this film that it would allow Majors to make the jump from television roles to being a movie star. But, while they were filming, his then wife, Farrah Fawcett began a much publicized affair with actor Ryan

O'Neal. It made for a rocky time for Majors, but he was contractually obligated to finish the film. Combined with the fact that this one ended up being financially unsuccessful, he ended up sticking with television, and no longer sought out leading man roles. It's a little bit *Mad Max*, a little *Death Race 2000*, but also a little bit of a buddy flick, but like, a really watered down version of all of those. It seems to take the most inspiration from *Max*, although to be fair, that film wasn't really that big of a hit over here and wasn't really a sensation until *The Road Warrior* came out, so it's unlikely it was trying to cash in on that. It was partially written by Christopher Crow, who would later go on to write *The Last of the Mohicans*, and the film was

built around his first draft, but was drastically rewritten. It ended up so far removed from his original concept that he had his name removed from the film, and as stated before, it didn't do that well when it was released. Critics didn't care for it, either, with most saying that the dramatic parts were dull and the action sequences? Well, they were dull too. In fact, this film's status as being something that's considered…not good…was cemented when it was riffed by the guys from MST3K in their very first season, when they were still a public access show.

M**y Rating - 2.** When I listed off the films that this one seems to be greatly inspired by, I would think that this is something that I would greatly enjoy, but instead I found it to be a little tedious. There's no aspect of this one that we have seen done somewhere else, and done livelier. Besides that, this brings up a bunch of interesting concepts in the beginning with all of the satirical elements about the world that these characters inhabit, but then the actual plot of the film ignores all of that. On the contrary, it goes a good deal out of its way to avoid discussing any of those things in favor or simply "plane chases car" set pieces. You can also tell that Majors was going through some things here, as his performance is a touch stilted. You can't say that about Meredith, though, who seems to having a grand old time up in that airplane.

C**ultural Significance - 2.** Even though this does have a touch more name recognition and a couple of noted stars involved, it's still just not widely seen. There was a short period where it got a decent amount of cable airings, but it was never one of the mainstays.

S**hould You Watch It?** Even though I didn't have much favorable to say about this one, it still has some fun chases, so I'd say yes? Besides, people other than me seem to enjoy it more, so perhaps give it a chance.

Sequel? No.

Remake? No.

QUICK RANK:

RATING -

CULTURAL SIGNIFICANCE -

Apr. 10th, '81
EXCALIBUR

Another entry on April 10th was *Excalibur*, one of the more prestigious releases in the fantasy genre. It starts with a big battle in the dark ages, and Merlin is here and agrees to get Excalibur from the Lady of the Lake, and you may be a little disappointed when her hand shows up and it's not holding a chainsaw. Merlin gives the blade to King Uther, who is one of the Usual Suspects (Gabriel Byrne), and Merls helps him use magic to bang his rival's hot wife, and they have a kid together, and that child is named Arthur. Shortly after, Uther is ambushed and killed, but in order to keep Excali from them, he buries it into a big rock, and Merlin says whoever draws it shall be the next king. Years later, the sword is still there and not even Picard (Patrick Stewart, of course) can pull it out, and he has mind powers, but they're better at making women's clothes fall off than pulling swords. Teenage Arthur is here and he just yanks that sucker out, quickly forms a crew and encounters the lovely Guinevere. And yeah, if you don't get it by now, this is a very serious version of the King Arthur and the Knights of the Round Table legend. It was directed by John Boorman who has a pretty spotty filmography. He's got some amazing stuff like *Deliverance* and *Hope and Glory*, but he also has *Zardoz* and *Exorcist 2,* which are amazing for completely different reasons. This was actually the first film he did after the disaster of *Exorcist 2* and it began as an attempt to do *Lord of the Rings*. A lot of the imagery and the set design came from concept art developed for that, but when the studio couldn't commit to the budget, it ended up getting repurposed into this, with a far lower budget. It was a tricky shoot, with the opening battle being particularly difficult to shoot. Twice, all the footage came out underexposed and completely useless, causing them to shoot it all a third time. It also has the outstanding Helen Mirren as Morgana and it was tricky putting her with Nicol Williamson, the actor who played Merlin. They had been in a stage show of Macbeth a while before this, and they had some difficulty getting along, to the point of refusing to speak to each other. However, while working on this film, whatever beef they had was fixed, and they ended up becoming good friends. Also, the role of Gawain is filled by a very young Darkman (Liam Neeson), very early on in his career. It was fairly expensive for the time, coming in at $11 million, but the reviews were consistently just mediocre. People lauded the scenery and all the visual aspects of the film, but criticized the direction, story, and lack of characterization. It did pretty well, though, taking in around $35 million, making it a hit. Also, it did manage to get an Oscar nomination for the cinematography, although it lost out to *Reds*.

My Rating - 3.5. This is a tough call because this movie is just a marvel to look at. Nearly every scene is stunningly gorgeous. It just manages to create this feeling of epicness that you're really not getting from any other film in this book. I think it's fair to say that when it comes to cinematography, there's a distinct difference between film and art. And this sways heavily into the art world of things since it's just so damn pretty. However, the plot…that's another story. It's just such a mess and Boorman may have been so involved in making things look good and not spending time with his actors, since the acting tends to come off as forced and overwrought. I've never really had the interest in the Arthurian legend that others have, so perhaps it's that I'm not externally invested in the story, but I will also admit that this movie doesn't really make me want to dive into it more. Damn good lookin', though.

Cultural Significance - 3.5. This gets a decent boost from the sheer level of talent and name recognition involved with it. Plus, it's a pretty well known work, even if not in a major blockbuster kind of way, and earned itself an Oscar nomination. However, it can't really get any higher since it never really pushed further into a mainstream relevance.

Should You Watch It? Absolutely. If you're familiar with Arthurian legend, it's interested to see it adapted. If you're not, it's a cool but flawed story that's told beautifully.

Sequel? No. 

Remake? No.
Although there's been other version of the Arthur legend.

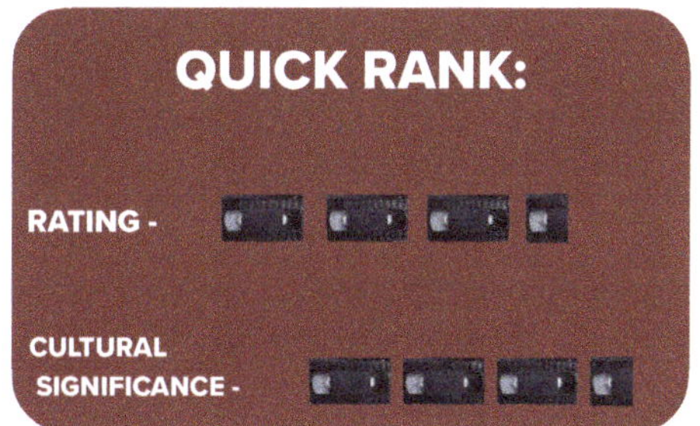

May 21st, '81
THE GIRL, THE GOLD WATCH AND DYNAMITE

This next little number is another TV movie and it first aired on May 21st, and it's *The Girl, The Gold Watch, And Dynamite*, and if that title sounds familiar, it's because this is a sequel to last year's *The Girl, The Gold Watch, And Everything*, which we covered just a little earlier in this book.

Now, in the first one, the character of Kirby was played by Robert Hayes, but how he's been recast. The same goes for his fiancée, formerly played by Pam Dawber. Zohra Lampert is back as Kirby's secretary, Wilma though and we find out that the watch that stops time works for 20 minutes a pop, can only be used 6 times in 24 hours and must be used once every 14 days or will stop working forever. When Bonnie gets a letter from her mother saying there's trouble on the farm she grew up on, they head up to Sacramento to help out, making sure to take the watch. It seems like there's issues with the levy and the farm could be flooded out at any time, and how about this? They go to see the farm and Bonnie's dad is there and he thinks they're trespassing and he literally shoots at them but Kirby stops time, and pushes the bullets out of the way. Keep in mind, her father is meant to be a gentle country boy, and they introduce him by having him almost murder people for simply daring to drive onto his property. The dad is Dr Nicholas Van Helsing (Jack Elam), and this one was originally titled *The Girl, The Gold Watch, And Everything Else*, but it was decided that that title may have been a touch too similar to the original and that people would think it was the same movie, so they substituted *Dynamite* in there instead. It was directed by Hy Averback, who had been working since the '50s, and only did a few more things after this, but one of those things was the comedy *Where The Boys Are*. 2001's Frank is here (Gary Lockwood), as does my girlfriend, Morgan Fairchild, yeah, that's the ticket, and of course, Jerry Mathers as the Beaver. Uh… Deputy Watts. When it turns out that the whole levy thing is all just a swindle to get Bonnie's parents off the land by some developers, shenanigans are kicked off, although it's all pretty low key. I suppose you could say that it at least has a little more plot than the first one?

My Rating - 2. Compared to the first one, at least this is a moderate step in the right direction? Like, at least they don't wait until the movie's almost over to use the damn watch. It's funny though, because it's like they still don't really want to use the watch, except in very specific situations. It was kinda like the old *Hulk* TV show, where you knew that he was going to change exactly two times per episode. Once would happen fairly early on, and then once again right near to end to wrap things up. This is the same. They need to use the watch at these specific moments in the script and then only use it in the most basic of ways. The concept of a watch that can stop time and has these weird, specific magic rules seems like it would be fascinating stuff, and it likely would be if they weren't more interested in silly hijinks of a sitcom level instead.

Cultural Significance - **1.** People are barely aware that there's a first one of these, let alone a sequel. You can't even boost this one due to having some star power, because the recasting eliminated all of that. I mean, Tom Poston shows up briefly, so if you're really hankering for *Mork & Mindy* cast members, I guess it has you partially covered.

Should You Watch It? I'd say no. It's a distinct step up from the first part, but not enough to earn it a recommendation.

Sequel? No.

Remake? No.

QUICK RANK:

RATING -

CULTURAL SIGNIFICANCE -

May 22nd, '81
OUTLAND

Ok. This next one is a bigger deal and on May 22nd, *Outland* was released. It sets us on a mining station in orbit around Io, a moon of Jupiter, and we see one of the miners have a psychotic break and tear open his spacesuit. The moon's Marshall, who named the dog Indiana (Sean Connery) is newly stationed there, and the mine's general manager is putting on the Ritz (Peter

Boyle). Shortly after, another also kills himself through decompression at the same time that Marshall O'Neil's wife unexpectedly heads back to earth, leaving him on his own. But then, when it seems like crew members losing their minds is occurring more and more frequently, they soon discover it's because they've been taking a new drug that increases their productivity rate but drives them insane. He soon discovers that the drugs are being supplied by Shepard and his own Sargent is in on it, and has to try to take the drug ring down on his own. This one was directed by Peter Hyams, who had already dipped his toes into the sci-fi world with *Capricorn One*, and would later do some stuff of varying degrees of quality, like 2010, *Timecop*, *Stay Tuned*, and *End of Days*. The film came about because he wanted to make a western but was told that westerns don't sell, so he made one anyone, but just set it in space. Instead of the western frontier, he

93

made it the final frontier, and was greatly influenced by the classic *High Noon*. It's not so much as to be a direct remake, but the inspiration is obvious. But it also took a good deal of its vibe from *Alien*, and considering that both films had the same producer, there's fan theories out there that place them in the same universe, since they both feature a shadowy corporation in charge of everything that's simply referred to as "The Company." However, there's a more direct link to the director's own work. The name of the mining company in the film is Con-Amalgamate, which is the same name as a company featured in *Capricorn One,* as well as an earlier feature called *T.R. Baskin*. That film would also feature Peter Boyle, and wasn't directed by Hyams, although he did the screenplay. The original title for this was actually *Io,* named after the moon it takes place on, but one of the higher ups on the production team said that people would confuse it for the number 10. When Hyams objected, they did a random experiment that showed the executive to be correct, so they changed the name. Upon release, it was met with mixed results. Reviews went either way, with some praising it, and others calling it dull and uninteresting. The box office went the same direction since it did well in the big cities, but failed to land with less populous areas, and would go on to make slightly more than it cost. The budget was $16 million, and its final take was around $20 million, which isn't really a disaster, but it's certainly not a success either. It did however, earn an Oscar nomination for best sound, although it lost to *Raiders of the Lost Ark*.

My Rating - 3.5. You know, I've never really been a Western fan. It's just never been a genre that hit for me, although there's been some that I've enjoyed. Like gangster movies, it's a whole subsegment that I completely get the appreciation for, but just doesn't much interest me. I do like this sort of subversion of the tropes and taking the concept of a western and tossing into space, though, and giving it that different backdrop increases the appeal. On the down side, though, it's just so damn dry. I've never been opposed to a slow pace, but this moves perhaps a touch too sluggish. Plus, since they went ahead and switched the setting to outer space, I would hope they would take advantage of that more, but it never really does much with it outside of the opening. It's like they wanted to do this sci-fi western thing, but didn't want to dip too far into either world.

Cultural Significance - 3. This one definitely was a bit more known, but it's not one that ever fully crossed over into mainstream success. But, it gets extra points for featuring a big cast of known names, the involvement of Hyams, and getting that Oscar nom.

Should You Watch It? Yes. This isn't exactly a solid slam dunk, but it's still absolutely worth the time.

Sequel? No.

Remake? No.

CLASH OF THE TITANS

This next one Is an epic and it came out on June 12th and it's *Clash of the Titans*, a movie that anyone with cable in the '80s has seen a million times. It begins with a King casting his daughter to the sea in an effort to prevent a prophecy, and Zeus is here, played by Laurence damn Olivier, classing things up, and Honey Ryder (Ursula Andress) is here too. Dame Maggie Smith steps in, and The king of the gods is pissed that Acrisius killed his daughter, and unleashes the Kraken to destroy his kingdom. Meanwhile, Danae's child grows up safely, and becomes Harry Hamlin, and look, if this were any other movie and I saw Harry Hamlin, I would call him Perseus, so here, that's what I'm gonna call him. He gets sent on a quest, but at least he has Micky in his corner (Burgess Meredith), and some gifts from Zeus like a helmet and sword and shield. His adventures have him encounter giant buzzards, the Pegasus, the twisted Calibos who I used to have an action figure of, and was the only one I had from this film so he fought Gi Joe a lot. He also gets the movie's breakout star, the clockwork owl, Bubo. The director on this one was Desmond Davis, and he was mostly a TV director and in fact, hadn't done a feature film for about 13 years before this. But, since he had done several Shakespeare films for the BBC, they thought he'd be the perfect fit for the role. Now, the special effects may look a bit outdated now, but they were the work of the legendary Ray Harryhausen, one of the great innovators of stop motion work. He created all the stop motion work on this one, including Calibos, the giant bird, the Pegasus, the Kraken, Medusa, and the scorpions. It would go on to become the final film to feature his work, since the advent of more advanced technologies made his work less desirable, leading him to retire. At one point in the process, the film was shopped to different studios, and one of the contenders was Orion Pictures, but they would only do it if Arnold Schwarzenegger took the lead, so no deal was made, since producer Charles Scheer didn't think he'd be able to handle the amount of dialogue necessary. The reviews were pretty favorable, with most critics enjoying it, although it did get its share of criticism as well, and it was fairly costly for the time period, with a budget of around 15 million. Unfortunately, it came out on the same day as *Raiders of the Lost Ark*, some tough competition, and only took the number 2 spot, but still did quite well overall. It earned around $40 million in the US and around $70 million worldwide, making it one of the biggest hits of the year. And I think it's because they all saw how amazing the stop motion Medusa was, because that thing is great. Besides, it had to also earn a ton of money from selling off the cable rights because this seemed to air on a loop back in the day.

My Rating - 4. And talk about nostalgia. I can't tell you how many times that I've seen this one. I might actually credit it for where some of my knowledge of mythology comes from, even if it's not the most accurate of depictions. I have some really fond memories of it, although I do have to admit that it doesn't really live up to all of those feelings. There's just a disjointedness to the story that feels a little too meandering and by the time we get to the finale where Perseus faces off against the Kraken, you're like, "oh, yeah, that's what he was doing." One thing that DOES hold up are those effects, though, because Harryhausen brought an air of magic to everything and really made them feel alive.

Cultural Significance - **4.5.** This is one that practically everyone knows. It's been widely seen and is well remembered, but also contains a fair amount of star power, and absolutely deserves some extra love for being the final feature work for the great Ray Harryhausen. You can also thank it for exposing the world to the expression, "Release the Kraken!"

Should You Watch It? By the gods, yes.

Sequel? No.

Remake? Yes. In 2010, there was a remake with the same title, directed by Louis Leterrier and featuring Sam Worthington in the Perseus role. It would have a follow up in 2012 called *Wrath of the Titans*, which was not quite as successful.

DRAGONSLAYER

June was a big month for sword and sorcery type flicks because a little later that month, on June 26th, *Dragonslayer* was released. The Supreme Being (Ralph Richardson) is a wizard and Janosz (Peter MacNicol) is his apprentice and a town that is beset upon by a dragon needs his help since he's the last sorcerer. In an effort to prove that he's as magical as he says, he allows himself to be stabbed, which of course, kills him. Galen is then left to deal with the problem on his own after he discovers his own magic abilities through the use of an amulet. The town has been sacrificing virgins to the dragon, and he discovers that Valerian is actually a girl posing as a boy to avoid being offered. When they think that he's stopped the dragon by sealing off its cave, they all celebrate, but it turns out to be premature when the beast returns as Galen loses his amulet. He's left to team up with Valerian to try to end the dragon's reign of terror and save the village, and this one was handled by Matthew Robbins, who has had a really interesting career. As a director, he's only done 8 things, with 5 being films. One was *Corvette Summer*, a comedy, then this fantasy film, *The Legend of Billie Jean* (fair is fair), *Batteries Not Included*, and then a movie called *Bingo* about a dog. But he's more prolific as a writer and has worked quite a bit with Stephen Spielberg, but also is a frequent collaborator with Guillermo Del Toro. It was a pretty large budget, costing $18 million to make, which is more than *Excalibur* or *Clash of the Titans*, the other two fantasy films of this year, and a large portion of that went to the dragon effects. It's said that a full quarter of the budget went to the making it come to life, using several different methods. There were large practical props, and miniature effects, and a new stop motion technique was created specifically for this film, called Go Motion. Instead of taking a picture of a still model and then moving it slightly and then taking another picture of it to simulate motion, here the model was mechanized to have slight movements. When the shots are taken, the minor motion is captured, and when put together, create a more smooth and fluid look for the movements as opposed to the standard stop motion. The dragon is often cited as the coolest part of the film, and both Guillermo Del Toro and *Game of Thrones* writer, George R R Martin have declared it to be the greatest dragon ever put on film. When released, critics embraced it and gave it glowing reviews, praising the effects and the story, but unfortunately audiences didn't react the same way. It only made $14 million at the box office, branding it a bomb, although over time it's become a cult classic. It did get nominated for an Oscar for the score, though, but lost out to Chariots of Fire, which I get because oh, great…now I have that theme in my head.

My Rating - 4. Who knew that 1981 was going to be such a thumper of a year for fantasy? Like *Clash*, this has some great stuff happening in it, but unlike that one, my attachment to this one doesn't have anything to do with nostalgia. I don't know if this was just on at times that I wasn't around, or if I just wasn't as interested in watching it, but this is a film I've only caught a couple of times, most of them recently. I do have to say that I wish that the pacing was a little stronger, because it does lag quite a bit in the middle of it all, but that's a minor quibble when you have that astonishing finale. The mixture of the practical stuff and the Go Motion may not exactly be the smoothest, but it still looks fantastic. When they said that this is one of the best dragons ever put on film, they absolutely weren't kidding, and it still holds up as looking amazing today.

Cultural Significance - 3.5. This gets some extra points for being decently known and remembered, but gets more points for its innovation. It advanced special effects quite a bit, creating new stop motion technology, and essentially putting Harryhausen out of business. However, it never really made it that big, so I can't place it much higher.

Should You Watch It? Yes. The story's still a treat and that dragon is absolutely banging.

Sequel? No.

Remake? No

QUICK RANK:

RATING -

CULTURAL SIGNIFICANCE -

So here's where this list is going to liven up, because on July 10th, we get the release of John Carpenter's *Escape From New York*. It did have a premiere in April, and also debuted in a few places earlier that summer, but July 10th is when it went wide. It gives us the far future of 1997, in which Manhattan is now a large prison that has been walled off and monitored. But when Air Force one is the subject of a hijacking, President Sam Loomis (Donald Pleasance) is launched in an escape pod that lands right in the heart of it. Fortunately, they had just arrested former war hero turned criminal, and all around rude guy, RJ Macready, or I mean Elvis, or I mean, Santa Claus, or wait, Jack Burton, no no wait. I got it. It's Snake Plissken (Kurt Russell), and he's given 24 hours to go in to New York City, retrieve the president and get him out or else a bomb goes off in his head. The always amazing Tom Atkins is here as well, as is the man who shot Liberty Valance (Lee Van Cleef). I actually don't think he did the shooting but you know what I mean. So of course, this is by John Carpenter, his follow to *The Fog*, and at this point, he was on a roll since *Halloween* was a major hit and *The Fog* did pretty well, too. And this script was something he had been sitting on since the '70s, and he wrote it in the wake of Watergate. The public was feeling pretty skeptical about the presidency, and this script reflected that. At the time, no one would produce it, but since he had now built up some clout, he was able to get it bankrolled. And here's a little tidbit: before they went into production, Carpenter became concerned that his version of the script was a little too straightforward of an action story, and was missing some of the more satiric elements that he thought the concept needed, so he brought in Nick Castle, the actor who portrayed Michael Meyers in the first *Halloween,* to help him out. Castle added in some comedic elements, created the character of Cabbie, and is responsible for the entire ending of the film. And then, the company funding the film weren't really keen on having Russell as the lead, considering he had just done a run of Disney productions and the comedy *Used Cars*, and they wanted a more distinct action leading man. They suggested someone like Charles Bronson for the gig, but Carpenter said that

Charlie was too old and wanted someone a little newer to the game. Of course, he also made a role for his then wife, Adrienne Barbeau, who had just made her theatrical debut one year earlier with *The Fog*. One of the more interesting "making of" aspects of the movie is the 3D model of the city displayed on a computer screen as Snake enters the city. At the time, computers were unable to do this kind of rendering and the effect was done practically, with a city model done in black with green outlines on the buildings. With a price tag of around 6 million, the film did quite well, bringing in around $25 million, cementing the director as a man who could deliver box office profits, if not mega blockbusters. The reviews were pretty favorable as well, with most critics praising its weirdness and satirical nature. Of course, a sequel happened, but not for another 15 years, and there's also been comic books and a game, marking Plissken's place in history. One silly tidbit about the tie ins is that there was a comic book crossover series that had Snake meet up with Jack Burton from *Big Trouble in Little China*, and established that they were simply alternate universe versions of each other.

M**y Rating - 4.5.** I think most people that know me know Carpenter is my favorite director. He himself claims this is his favorite of his films, and I don't agree, but it's in his top 3. It's such a great concept, and was unique at the time. And I know that it's easy to identify Russell with this type of character at this point, but before this, he was known for brighter and more cheerful character, but he just slipped into Snake like he slid into those camo pants.

C**ultural Significance - 4.5.** There's no denying the influence this had on the genre. It gave birth to copycat films, gave us one of cinema's defining anti-heroes, and featured a roster of genre stars. Not to mention it's a Carpenter film, one of the genre's premiere auteurs. This is clearly one of the biggies, although it's not quite in the cultural eye enough to be a full five.

S**hould You Watch It?** Yes. You have 24 hours to do so, or the bomb in your head will explode.

Sequel? Yes. 15 years later, in 1996, *Escape From L.A.* was released. A third entry, entitled *Escape From Earth* was planned, but after the 2nd film was a commercial failure, it was scrapped.

Remake? No, although it's been attempted several times, the first being in 2007 with Gerard Butler playing Snake. Much later, in 2017, Robert Rodriguez was announced to give it a shot, and later it was stated that the team Radio Silence were now directing, although that version appears to also be in production limbo. Recently, though, it was hinted that version would not be a remake, and instead would be a sequel.

QUICK RANK:

RATING -

CULTURAL SIGNIFICANCE -

Jul 11th, '81
SCHOOL IN THE CROSSHAIRS

A mere one day later, on July 11th, we're headed to japan for *School in the Crosshairs*, and it looks like it also had the title, *The Aimed School*. It's set at a school with a young girl named Yuka, and a very excitable teacher who likes to bang his fist on the table. Yuka has a reputation for being the smartest kid in class which makes some

people dance, and everyone just loves her. She also discovers that she possesses powers and reverses time to save a small child from being run over. She also has a guy friend who has a pet monkey, and really, I would love a pet monkey, but I also like having my face not torn off. She eventually uses her powers to help her guy Seki win his tournament, which isn't really the most heroic thing to do, like isn't that cheating really? But then she notices a strange man watching her who exhibits magical powers and tells her that she could rule the world if she wished. But, then things get weird when a new girl arrives as school, and she has powers of her own, and immediately has beef with Yuka. Pretty soon, she's creating these fascist style school patrols, all in matching uniforms and rounding up any students that they consider to be exhibiting bad behavior, with things escalating to the evil girl showing up in a red leotard to attack to the gym teacher. Every time she uses her powers, it's represented by everything turning grey, and if this seems a little oddball and surreal, consider that it's from Nobuhiko Obayashi, the director of the infamous *House*. You may have heard of that one as *Hausu*, as it's often referred to, probably to avoid confusion with the Steve Miner film, but it's his most revered work and if you haven't seen it, then you haven't seen the weirdest film of all time. He did this one shortly afterwards, and you can see some of his trademark eccentricities in it, mainly in the experimental visuals going on, even if the plot itself is more straightforward. It's definitely a "message" movie since it's about the rise of fascism as how easily people can get wrapped up in a charismatic dictator, just on a school level, but it's also an example of what's referred to in japan as an "idol" movie. Basically, it's when a young actor becomes super famous really quickly and a movie is made to basically promote them as a person as much as possible to broaden their appeal, as opposed to an actor playing a role as a character. It's simply them being themselves, more or less, which really isn't different than what's done everywhere, but they just have a name for it and acknowledge it. By the ending, it's gone full weird, with space battles and an overdose of low grade and awesome effects and people trapped in stars.

My Rating - 3.5. Man, there's a lot going on in this movie. There's just a whole jumble of plots and themes and they're thrown together here and everyone just crosses their fingers and hopes that it all comes together. And it kinda does? But it mostly doesn't, and it's all muddled as far as a story goes, but in the end, it doesn't matter. It has this charm to it and a ton of heart, so you forget all that and just go along for the ride, especially once the psychedelics kick in and everything starts to feel like a fever dream. If you've seen Hausu, then you'll have a certain expectation in terms of goofiness, and this WILL scratch that itch, but it doesn't quite go the distance, so if you always thought that movie was just too weird, then you'll likely get more pleasure out of this one.

Cultural Significance - **1.5.** This is another one that is very likely to have a bigger relevance in its native country, but not as much here in the States. Here, it's virtually unknown and is mainly just something that would show up as "that *House* guy's other movie."

Should You Watch It? Yeah, this is worth it. Put this one in YOUR crosshairs.

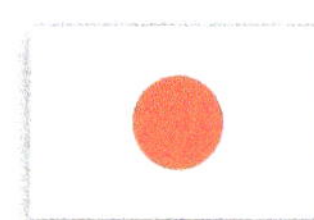

Sequel? No.

Remake? Yes.
Although it can also just be described as an alternate adaptation of the source novel. In 2012, an animated film called *Psychic School Wars* told the same story, but a more straightforward version.

Aug 7th, '81
HEAVY METAL

The volume was turned up on August 7th with the epic release of *Heavy Metal*. It kicks off in the best way possible as an astronaut descends to Earth in a Corvette to the sounds of "Radar Rider." That astronaut then opens a case with a glowing green orb that kills him and begins to tell his daughter that it's the Loc Nar and it tells her stories, in which it is the primary objective of the

109

characters. And if you're not aware, *Heavy Metal* is a comic magazine from France known as *Metal Hurlant* in France and licensed here. It's been running since 1977 and features an anthology of science fiction stories, mostly with an adult bent. The film is the same thing, adapting some of the more popular tales from the title, adding the framing sequence and presence of the Loc Nar to bridge them together. The first is called "Harry Canyon", based on a Moebius tale, and has John Candy showing up to lend his voice, and is a futuristic take on a film noir, with the original comic said to have inspired the look of *Blade Runner*. The second tale is an adaptation of Richard Corben's sci fi sword and sorcery epic, "Den". Candy also shows up here as the title character and it's essentially a kind of Conan in space. The third story is based on a character from Swamp Thing legend Bernie Wrightson called "Captain Stern" and has an assortment of *SCTV* stars, including Eugene Levy as Stern and Joe Flaherty as his lawyer and also has John Vernon as the judge. Next is a World War 2 zombie tale that's an original tale from Dan O'Brannon, then "So Beautiful and So Dangerous," a tale of aliens and robots arriving on Earth , based on an Angus McKie tale from the comic. That one also has Candy, Levy, and Flaherty but also adds Harold Ramis in there. The final sequence is probably the most iconic and it's "Taarna," based on another Moebius tale, although it differs quite drastically and it's more of an inspiration for as opposed to an adaptation. It has the introduction of the warrior woman Taarna, who is featured on the film's poster. Each section had a different team with a variety of writers and directors, and it was produced by *Ghostbusters* director Ivan Reitman. It used a variety of different animation techniques, handled by different teams, allowing for a quicker turnaround time for the sequences, and got mixed reviews. Audiences liked it though and it was a modest hit, landing $20 million at the box office, against a budget of $9 million. Home releases got a bit tricky though, since there were some legal issues with the song featured in the film. Some of the contracts were only for the theatrical release of the film, so when it came time for the home release, they were unable to use those songs. It wasn't until 1996 that it got a proper release with the original music, thanks to *Teenage Mutant Ninja Turtle* co creator Kevin Eastman. He purchased the rights to the magazine, and reached a settlement with the rights holders of the songs, allowing it to be delivered to the VHS world and beyond.

My Rating - 3.5. Pretty sure that I wasn't supposed to watch this, but I found a way to do it anyway. There's definitely a solid amount of nostalgia attached to seeing this, but it doesn't quite live up to my memory. And probably the thing that holds it up the most is the animation. Compared to others from this same time period, it often looks stiff and low rent, which is a sharp contrast to how elegantly illustrated that the book versions were. Plus, the quality level of the stories within are uneven, and often feel like they're rushing to cram a much bigger tale into a ten to fifteen minute framework.

Cultural Significance - 3. I'm pretty sure this is a somewhat commonly seen film, and it's fondly remembered, but never broke into the mainstream and wasn't able to maintain its level of relevance. Plus, I think that the magazine itself was where the relevance stems from.

Should You Watch It? Yes. And turn it up.

Sequel? Yes. In 2000, the appropriately titled *Heavy Metal 2000* was released, although it's not as well remembered.

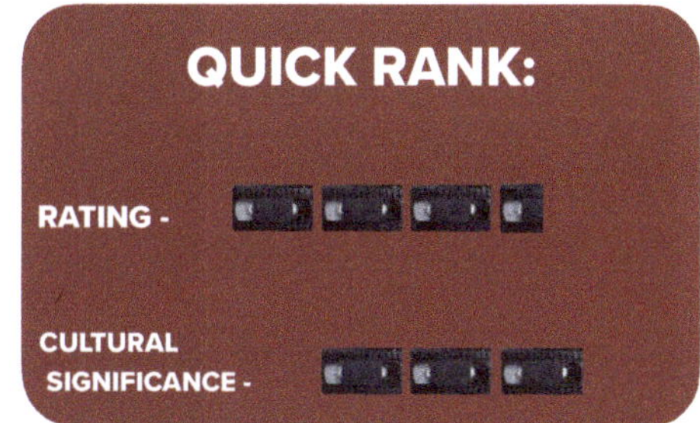

Remake? In a way. There's been talks about doing a reboot of the film since 2008, although they always seem to get waylaid, although one of those attempts ended up getting retooled and retitled, becoming the Netflix series *Love, Death and Robots*. There was also a 2 season live action version in France called *The Metal Hurlant Chronicles* that featured some name talent and a decent budget, although that's likely more an alternate version of the book, as opposed to a remake of the film.

QUICK RANK:

RATING -

CULTURAL SIGNIFICANCE -

Aug 7th, '81
CONDORMAN

On that very same day, we also saw the premiere of *Condorman*, which has a guy named Woody Wilkins in a Condorman outfit ready to fly, while Teen Wolf's dad takes pictures. His flight doesn't go so well, and we find out that he's not exactly a superhero, he's a comic book artist who is obsessed with making a real, working suit. See, he's so committed to having his book be realistic, he doesn't want to have his character do anything that's not feasible in real life. His friend Harry is actually a low level member of the CIA and he has to choose a civilian to do a simple drop and he enlists Woody. He excitedly agrees and meets up with his contact, a Bond girl (Barbara Carrera), although she's not what she seems as she's working for either Dr Heckyl or Mr Hype (Oliver Reed). Word of Condorman as a secret agent spreads, so they need Woody's help, and he reluctantly agrees so that he can meet up with Natalia. This was a live action venture from Disney, who were having a rough time in '81 with live action. They just had a couple of busts, including *Dragonslayer*, so they were hoping a wacky superhero spy flick could turn things around. It was based on a novel called *The Game of X* that was more adult oriented than the Mouse's regular fare, and the film was considered a touch more risqué than normal, which is funny when you watch it now, as it's super tame, but apparently Carrera's sexiness was too much to contain. Charles Jarrot was brought on to direct, and he'd been in the business since the 60's and even won a Golden Globe in 1970 for *Anne of the Thousand Days*. He wasn't known for light comedy, though, so this was out of his normal scope. It's far less a superhero story than you would think, and for a good chunk, feels like a James Bond spoof with disguises and gadgets and cool cars like the Condormobile, which I distinctly remember having a Hot Wheels version of. But when I looked it up, it seems like it didn't exist, but I could swear I had some sort of toy version of it. The budget wasn't crazy, but it did cost $14 million, which was a decent price tag. I mean, *Dragonslayer*, which looks a good deal more expensive, only cost

$18 million, so it certainly wasn't made on the cheap. Unfortunately, it was met with some pretty negative reviews, calling it dull and uninteresting. That translated into lack of interest at the ticket booths as well, making only around $5 million, marking it as a flop, but it's since developed a decent sized cult following, especially with Disney fans. Because of that, there's been minor nods to the character in some Disney products, including his wings appearing in the *Disney Infinity* series of games and an appearance, in toy form, in one of the *Toy Story* short films. I guess I should also point out that he only appears in the Condorman uniform in the last 10 minutes or so of the movie and everything before that is low grade spy stuff, so if you're expecting a winged superhero adventure, you're gonna be disappointed.

My Rating - 3. Do you remember a sentence ago when I said that those expecting a superhero adventure were going to be disappointed? Well, that was me. If you're giving me a title like *Condorman* and showing me a dude with wings on the poster, then that's what I want. Although to be fair, the poster does mainly show him in a spy looking suit, so maybe I should have known. Perhaps it wouldn't have mattered if the spy parts of the film were really fun, and they're not. But they are *kinda* fun. This is still an enjoyable film and its absolutely not without merit, but it's also the kind of thing that doesn't stand out. There were plenty of James Bond ripoffs flying around at this point, so those aspects of the film don't stand out at all. The whole superhero goofball parts do, but they're unfortunately too little of this film.

Cultural Significance - 2.5. There's a certain amount of relevance that is pre baked into a film as soon as it's a part of the Disney oeuvre. Mainly because they're gonna make sure that it's known to the public through a deluge of marketing. And even though this isn't something that you saw plastered everywhere, they definitely made people aware that it existed.

Should You Watch It? Yes. It's still a good time, but it's also fairly forgettable.

Sequel? No.

Remake? No

QUICK RANK:

RATING -

CULTURAL SIGNIFICANCE -

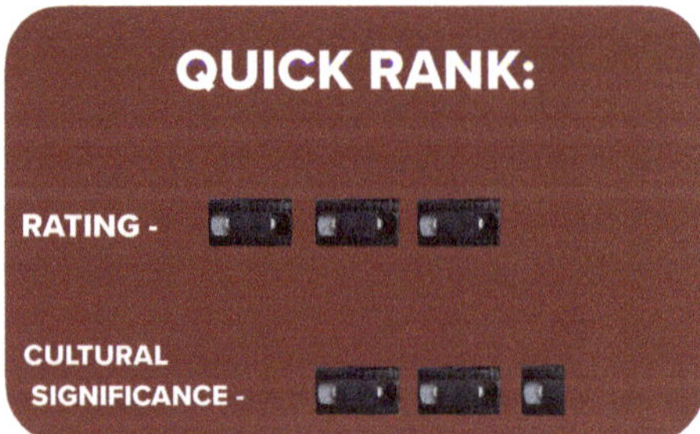

FIREBIRD 2015 A.D.

Next up, we head to September 18th for *Firebird 2015 AD*, and it's set in the far off future of 2015. Much like in *The Last Chase*, it seems like gasoline is in tight supply, only being supplied to the authority figures. Ralphie's dad (Darren McGavin) is here, and he's something called a "burner", someone who defies the government order and continues to drive a car. The group hunting them are the DVC, the Department of Vehicle Control. Red has a son named Cam and they have a strained relationship, but he also has a glorious Pontiac Firebird Transam, and yeah, this really does feel like *The Last Chase*. Future where gas is rationed out. Drivers not allowed. One man decides to take his souped up car out with a younger man as his passenger. They even feature an actor in common with George Touliatos. All they need is Burgess Meredith and his airplane! Instead we get Troy McClure, or sorry, Doug McClure, as part of the DVC, but one of their number has gone over the edge and is blowing burners up, which causes dissension in the ranks. Meanwhile, young Cam flirts with another burner named Jill, sparking his interest in cars. And this was directed by David Robertson, who had a unique career. He directed four things in the span of a decade, with this being his first feature, and then did an anthology segment in '86, and then two TV movies. But, outside of directing, he has a huge filmography of other work, including first assistant director roles and production manager jobs. He worked on some horror classics like the original *Black Christmas, Friday the 13th part 5*, and *Return of the Living Dead*. There's also this weird focus on dad getting his son laid and also a strange number of musical interludes. This was a Canadian venture, and although it debuted on the 8th in the US, then went to the Canadian market a week later, on the 18th. It wasn't warmly received, and didn't make any impact on the market, and ended up on a couple of worst movies of all time lists, although I'm gonna questions those lists, since it's really not all that terrible.

My Rating - 2. I said this wasn't terrible and I know that a 2 is not exactly a great rating, but it's a far cry from one of the worst films of all time.

Sure, it's on the dull side and doesn't do much for most of its runtime, but it has a handful of entertaining bits.

Cultural Significance - **1.5.** This one is all but forgotten, didn't make a splash at the time, but it does feature a few recognizable faces.

Should You Watch It? Maybe if you're super into cars?

Sequel? No.

Remake? No

Sept 19th, '81
THRESHOLD

One day later, on September 19th, in Canada, there was the premiere of *Threshold*. It didn't get a US release until much later, though, not arriving here until 1983. We're in LA and meet Doctor President Snow (Donald Sutherland), and Mayor Ebert (Michael Lerner) is one of his patients, and he's approached for a former one played by Mare

Winningham. His wife is Sharon Acker, who we just saw not that long ago in *Happy Birthday To Me*, and when Doc Vrain goes to a heart transplant conference he runs into Seth Brundle (Jeff Goldblum), and they discuss the concept of doing an artificial heart. An interesting thing is that this takes place before a successfully transplanted artificial heart had been done. That didn't happen until 1982, and that's why you may be sitting there, looking at this film and saying "This doesn't seem like a science fiction film," as a medical drama, but it's actually the core definition of science fiction. It's taking a scientific principle and expanding upon it and elaborating to make a fictional tale. When making this, an actual heart transplant was a fictional concept, just one that was shortly rendered reality. So, when it looks like there's no other options for Carol, they decide to go ahead with the artificial heart and have her become the first human with one. And the director was

Richard Pearce who had previously done some TV, and one other film, but would go on to a long, eclectic career, including the Steve Martin film, *Leap of Faith*. He seems to have retired from directing, but still does producing and cinematography, including the Oscar nominated documentary, *Food Inc*. *Threshold* was a Canadian production, and even though it's set in the US, was filmed almost entirely in Ottawa, with a budget of around $5 million Canadian and went on to be highly acclaimed. It was nominated for 10 Genie awards, the Canadian equivalent of the Oscars, and won 2. Donald Sutherland took Best Actor, and it also got Best Cinematography, but lost out on Best Picture to *The Grey Fox*. Minor note but Sutherland and Goldblum had already worked together 3 years earlier in the *Invasion of the Body Snatchers* remake.

My Rating - 3. This is an interesting concept, and the performances are all top notch, but I'll admit that the story itself is pretty dry. And for a drama, it's not really all that dramatic.

Cultural Significance - **2.** It may not be spoken of all that much, but it did win a number of awards and has top talent involved. Also, it's not totally relevant to a sci-fi genre, when it no longer really fits it.

Should You Watch It? If your view of sci-fi is spaceships and lasers, then likely not, but it's worth checking out.

Sequel? No.

Remake? No

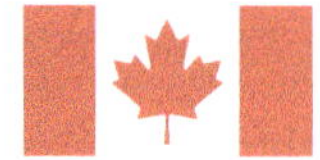

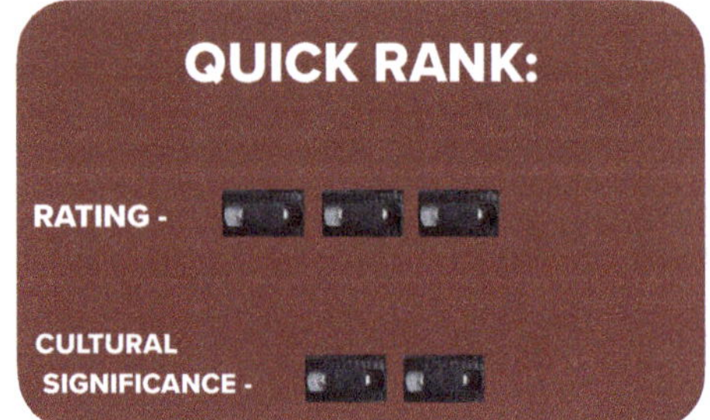

Oct ???, '81
WAR OF THE WORLDS : NEXT CENTURY

This next one is a bit of an odd one and played some time in October in Chicago at a film festival, but didn't get a regular release until February of 1983 in Poland. We find out that around the end of the century, Earth was contacted by aliens from Mars with the intention of helping to advance the human race. They're fed information from a propaganda like news program, although the anchor, Iron Idem, hates simply reading off stock scripts. The next day, he's visited by an aggressive police squad that destroy his house and kidnap his wife. Suddenly, his station is running blood drives and it seems as if the martians aren't as friendly as everyone is making out. It becomes apparent that the state is working with the martians and hiding their nefarious intentions, and fooling the general public. Idem buckles under the pressure and goes along with his state messaging, but one night he ends up in a type of shelter that turns out to be a concentration camp, and he sees how willing people are to simply obey the orders and not question when the police start doing things considered extremely abusive. He finally reaches his breaking point and realizes that fighting back is the only option, but turning the tide of public perception isn't easy when people are so resistant to change, so he faces an uphill battle. This is from Piotr Szulkin, a Polish director who mainly did work in his home country, and passed away back in 2018 but spent most of his earlier life in film, then switched to becoming a film school professor in the latter half of his life. And remember how I said that this film played in 1981, but then didn't get a regular release until 2 years later. Well, that's because it was banned. You see, as you can probably tell by the title, this was his take on the H.G. Wells novel, *War of the Worlds*, but he wanted a more modern, subversive take on the subject. So he constructed this tale, making it a critique of totalitarianism and television as a source of propaganda. But the problem was, at this particular time in Poland, there was a big government turmoil, leading to General Jaruzelski declaring martial law in the country, locking it down. This film, seen as a critique of the very thing that was occurring, was immediately banned and wouldn't be allowed to be released until the state of emergency was lifted, in 1983.

My Rating - 4. I'll admit that this film is a bit on the slow side, and it perhaps takes a little too long to get to the point of it all, but beyond that, it's a damn powerful film. I try not to dig too deep into current politics because there's a core contingency of the audience out there that get really upset hearing any traces of a political stance they don't agree with, but this film is amazingly relevant today. And the thing that downright breaks my heart is that the people that need to see this movie will likely see the propaganda machine as the opposite side of the spectrum from themselves. One thing that deserves a special call out is the performance by Roman Wilhelmi as Idem, as he really goes for it here, and considering he's on screen for about 90% of the movie, you need his performance to work. And it does. It truly does.

Cultural Significance - 2. Chalk this one down as another one that likely has a greater relevance in its home country, but just isn't all that known over here, but it does have a historical impact.

Should You Watch It? Absolutely. Watch it. Let the message soak in. Just replace the aliens with rich assholes in your mind. Oh, and don't expect to see Tom Cruise running away from any fireballs.

Sequel? No.

Remake? No

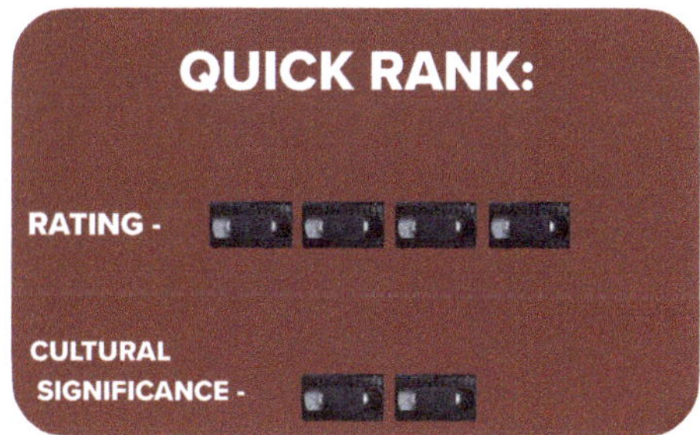

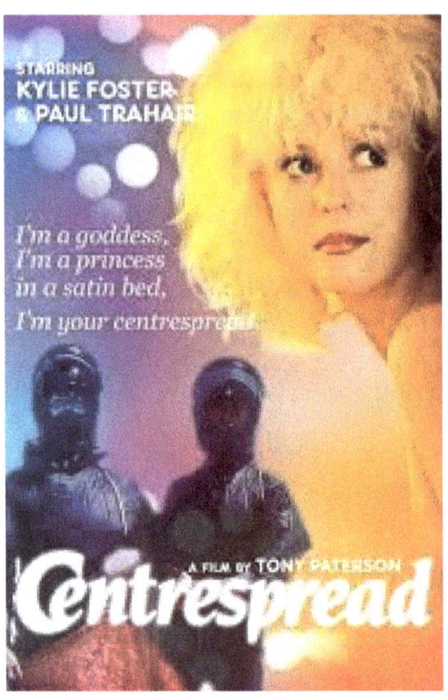

Oct 15th, '81
CENTRESPREAD

We're staying international, and on the 15th in Australia, we're checking out *Centrespread*. Based on the title, you'd assume it's about nude photography, and sure enough, it begins with a shoot involving a bald couple, breasts, blades, and it's 8 minutes in before you can even figure out what the hell is going on. It's set in the future and a guy named Gerard is a fashion photographer and the shoots are all kinda surreal, but it seems like his publishers are now looking for someone with a new look to spice things up. He goes out and about and happens to run into Niki working at a shop, and she's played by Kylie Foster, in one her earliest roles. She's not really known here, but has consistently been in Australian productions. There's then more photo shoots that are increasingly strange, and several moments in which the film sort of dances around just becoming standard porn, with long, leering shots of body parts that I think represent like, what the photographer is capturing and his primary interest, but then it's also just kinda like, "Here's some boobs." Gerard entices Niki into his world, and Tony Paterson is the director on this, but it was the only film in which he took that role. Most of his filmography consists of editing work and he cut some solid flicks, mostly Australian, and did the original *Mad Max*. This came out in the middle of the whole Ozploitation thing, although this one had a bit more emphasis on the 'ploitation part of things. The budget is apparently disputed, since there's reports that it cost $600k, but that seems unlikely. The production studio at the time said they intended to shoot 6 films for 1 million dollars, and this was one of them, so it'd put the budget at less than $200k. Then, a later interview with a producer claimed it was even less, and more likely between 125-150k. It was shot on 16mm and blown up, which was rare for a film with a budget like this, but does create that grainier look throughout the flick, but it's weird, because the futuristic setting doesn't come into play frequently. Based on the clothing and technology and stuff, it's clear it's meant to BE in the future, but you could easily had this set in present day and not much would change. There's not much plot to speak of. It's literally just a series of photo shoots in odd surroundings, as Gerard's work becomes less violent and aggressive and more about romance and love. It got pretty terrible reviews when it came out, even being called atrocious in local newspapers.

My Rating - 1.5. I wouldn't say that it's atrocious, but there's really not much to it. There's this nugget of an interesting story of the photographer toning his work down through his romantic attachment, but it's lost in the long softcore sequences.

Cultural Significance - 1. This one is practically completely unknown and is rarely talked about. Beyond that, it doesn't have any notable names and left no discernible impact on the genre.

Should You Watch It? This is one that's easy to pass on, unless you just want some eye candy on in the background.

Sequel? No.

Remake? No

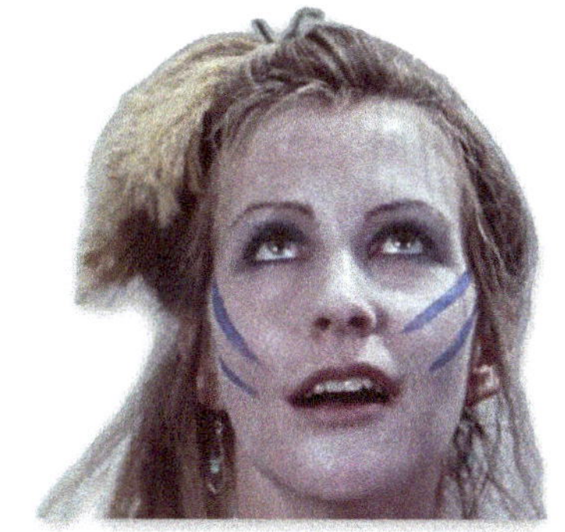

Oct 30th, '81
LOOKER

On October 30, one day before Halloween, a non horror flick was released in the form of one of the most prophetic films, *Looker*. It has the Big Fish (Albert Finney) as a plastic surgeon who is asked to perform surgery on a stunning commercial actress, based upon specifications that she's been given for perfection. Shortly after, though, here's someone in her apartment and bright flashes that seem to disorient her, causing her to from her balcony. Doc Roberts then sees a Partridge (Susan Dey), and it turns out that two of his former patients are dead, with objects placed in their apartments to make him look like a suspect. Another patient who warns him of a conspiracy that's killing the perfect girls is then murdered in a spectacular stunt, so he starts to investigate which leads him to one of the Magnificent Seven (James Coburn). Roberts starts to tag along with Cindy since she's the likely next target, which brings him face to face with Bernie Lomax (Terry Kiser). We find out a company is scanning the models into their computers, where they can then reproduce their likeness and pay them 200k per year, but then they're killing them. The Doc's search is blocked by Mustache Man, and that's his actual credit in the movie. He's listed as "Mustache Man," but he's also armed with the Looker gun, the source of those bright flashes. When you get zapped by it, you go into a sort of trance, making you lose track of time. The director on this, as well as the writer, is none other than Michael Crichton, author of a huge string of successful novels including *Jurassic Park*, *The Andromeda Strain*, and like,100 other books that movies have been made out of. Seriously, out of his 28 novels, half have been made into feature films, which is probably a lower ratio than Stephen king, but may actually have a higher box office total. Before this, he directed the original *Westworld*, *Coma*, and *The Great Train Robbery*, all of which he also wrote the screenplays for. At the time, *Looker* featured the first ever use of a CGI human character, although it's not necessarily used as an effect here and is more just showing the scanning of Cindy, so in this case the digital character is

meant to be a digital character instead of convincing you it's real. The weirdest thing is just how accurately this film predicted something is going on right now. Currently, the industry is extremely concerned about the studios wanting to use AI to replicate and recreate actors from their scanned likenesses, only without paying them 200k a year like in this movie. This film predicted a world where corporations would find living actors disposable once they were able to recreate their images, over 40 years before it actually happened. One actor that wasn't happy with being replaced, or at least, deleted, was James Coburn. He complained that a large number of his scenes ended up on the cutting room floor, which he said expanded the story of the film and improved it. From what I can tell, it's mainly one scene, but it's pretty long and it's basically one of those "villain shows up to explain his evil plan things and then leaves the heroes in a scenario they can easily escape." I can see why it was cut, but it does tie up a couple of loose ends in the overall story. It was a fairly pricey picture with people stating it cost anywhere from 8 to 12 million bucks, but flopped at the box office, bringing in a mere 3 million.

My Rating - **4.** Oh, look, it's another film that I can't deny that nostalgia plays a huge part in my rating. I loved this movie when I was younger and I still dig it just as much. There's just such interesting concepts going on here, from the CG replacements and the Looker gun itself, it's bringing up some unique stuff, even if it never really digs into them as much as you'd like them to. That's not to say that it doesn't dig in, because there's certainly some exploration of these themes, but it tends to focus more on the fun action side.

126

Cultural Significance - **3.5.** I might be over evaluating this one a touch, considering that it was a failure at the time and only reached people through constant cable runs, but those runs WERE constant. It also had Crichton at the wheel, a great cast, and is substantially more relevant today than ever.

Should You Watch It? Yes, but make sure to wear your special sunglasses when you do.

Sequel? No.

Remake? No

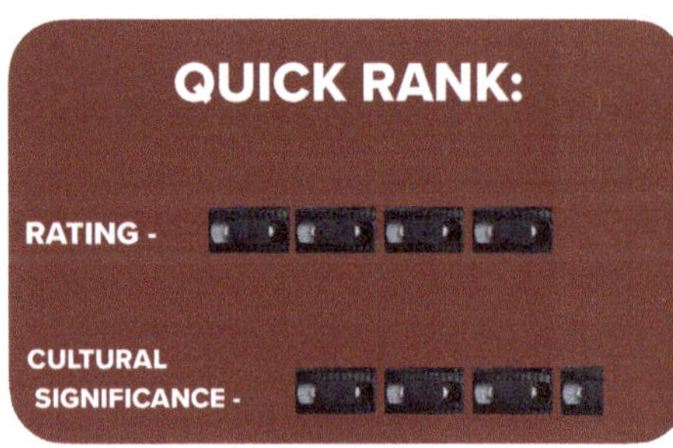

Oct 30th, '81
SHOCK TREATMENT

On that same day, another curiosity arrived in the form of a sort of sequel that everyone wanted…just not like this, and it's *Shock Treatment*. This is a weird one. There's this town named Denton, and the whole place is a TV studio and if you live here, you're either on a show, work on one, or are an audience member. There's a couple here that aren't happy about living there and it's Jessica Harper from *Suspiria* and Cliff De Young from like, everything. Their names are Brad and Janet, and if Brad and Janet from Denton sounds familiar, then you've seen *The Rocky Horror Picture Show* and we'll get back to that. B and J are unhappy together and their marriage is on the rocks, so they're chosen to participate on a game show called "Marriage Maze." Because of it, they're sent to other shows, with Brad being sent to "Dentonvale", which features one of the Dangerous Brothers (Rik Mayall). At Dentonvale, there's a brother/sister doctor combo and it's Riff Raff and Magenta (Richard O'Brien and Patricia Quinn), another link to *Rocky Horror*, although important to note that Brad and Janet don't recognize them. Oh, by the way, the host is played by Barry Humphries, who you probably know more as dame Edna, is on hand as well. And yeah, now for the obvious. This was intended as a follow up to *The Rocky*

Horror Picture Show, with Jim Sharman back to direct and Richard O'Brien again writing and starring. But, it's a strange combo of returning actors as new characters, and returning characters played by new actors. Seems Susan Sarandon wanted more money than they could afford, and Barry Bostwick wasn't available, so Harper and De

Young were brought on board to fill their roles. The only person from *Rocky* to play the same character was Jeremy Newson as Ralph Hapschatt, although his character seems different. So, because of these casting quirks and character differences, some don't actually consider this a sequel but can be seen either way. While there is continuity, there's enough wiggle room that it doesn't have to be either. And you know, for how beloved that rocky horror was, this was met with one hell of a backlash. Fans were angry that none of the lead actors returned, particularly Tim Curry, and hated that O'Brien refused to peg down exactly what the film was. The pre hype told people it wasn't a sequel, wasn't a prequel, but was an equal, which didn't tell them much. Critics didn't care for it either with their appreciation going towards the songs and set design, but saying the story was garbage. O'Brien agreed, later referring to it as an abortion. *Rocky Horror* was considered a flop when it came out, and slowly built its audience in midnight screenings, so this was never given a regular release and only went to the midnight circuit. Since the budget, compared to *Rocky* was double, the stakes were higher, but audiences didn't show up, and it vanished pretty quickly.

My Rating - 3. This may be controversial, but this just doesn't really bowl me over. I have some friends that are into this one as much as its predecessor, but I just don't buy into that. It's just too all over the place and never really knows what it wants to be. *Rocky Horror* was probably equally chaotic, but it still felt measured and thought out. That's not to say that it's not a good time, though. The overall look of it is really well done, and the world it creates seems as carefully crafted as the script isn't. Plus, the music is top notch, and even if there's nothing as iconic and catchy as "Time Warp," there's still plenty that you'll be humming in your head afterwards. Finally, though, even though I feel like this shouldn't be points off, but the absence of Curry does feel like this giant, gaping empty spot in the film. No one in this tale matches him as an actor or character in terms of levels of charm and charisma.

Cultural Significance - 3. Even though this is a sequel to an iconic film that became a massive phenomenon, this one more or less fell by the wayside. It has a cult following and it's significance is likely a little higher now, but it was never any sort of hit film and even fans of *Rocky Horror* will admit that its skippable. However, it gets a little extra boost for modern relevance, as its themes seemed to predict reality TV and TV obsessiveness.

Should You Watch It? Yes. Lot of fans out there have a higher opinion of this than me, and you may be one of them.

Sequel? No.

Remake? No

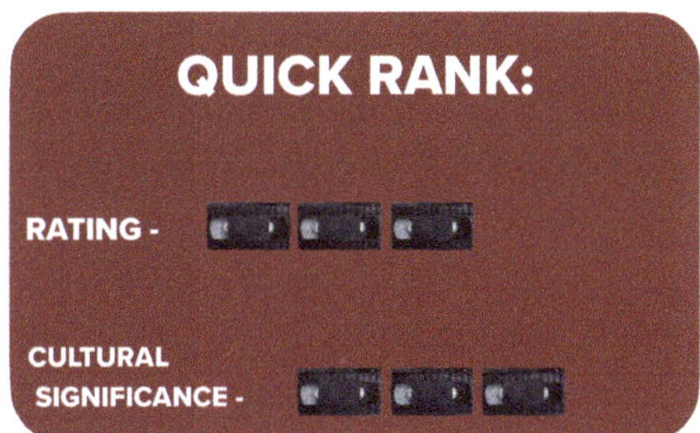

TIME BANDITS

A few days later, on November 6th, a film that I absolutely adore came out with *Time Bandits* and I have a lot to say about this one. We meet little Kevin who is obsessed with reading about history while his parents can't stop watching TV, and jeez with these last three movies, are we noticing a theme here? Everyone in the early '80s seemed to think that television was going to be the end of everything, but little did they know that this little thing called the internet was gonna take care of all that. There's a TV presenter that's mainly interested in the greater good (Jim Broadbent) THE GREATER GOOD, and that night, a knight on horseback bursts through Kevin's room. The next evening, he's ready for it, and prepped to take a photo, but instead a group of little people come through led by Randall, played by the brilliant David Rappaport. And look, I'm not trying to start this off on a down note or anything, but I find this depressing because of the group of actors that played the diminutive Bandits, only one remains alive. They're being pursued by a giant floating head looking for a map, but escape into Napoleonic France. They do so with a map of time that they say was stolen from the Supreme Being, and I know that Napoleon has a reputation for being short, but who knew he was a Hobbit (Ian Holm)? The director here was Terry

Gilliam, *Monty Python* alumni, and he had recently kinda struck out on his own as an artist. He was most known for doing those crazy animations in the episodes, and was trying to find funding for his pet project, *Brazil*. Unable to do that, he was able to get money from none other than George Harrison, who funded this as a family film, which uh…I guess? His fellow Pythoner, Michael Palin, cowrote the screenplay, and they set about their tale, which also featured Palin along with Olive Oyl (Shelley Duvall). It's also got John Cleese and my absolute favorite joke, which probably needs to be seen to capture the delivery, but he asks Strutter, one of the Bandits how long he's been a robber, and he replies "4 foot 1." And that part is hilarious but it's Cleese's retort of "4 foot 1? That is a long time" that really gets me. It's also got the amazing David Warner as the villainous Evil, Zardoz himself (Sean Connery) as King Agamemnon, and you also have Mona (Katherine Helmand) as an Ogre's wife on a pirate looking ship and man, do I have a story about that ship. You see, the boat they used is a replica of a Spanish galleon, built by a father/son team in the '60s into the '70s. It was used in the movie, and afterwards they changed the name of the boat to The Time Bandit. It gave tours in Newport Beach for a while, but then was purchased and sent to Big Bear Lake as a tour boat, where I got to ride it. Problem is: the tour guide mentioned that it was in the movie, and then called *Time Bandits* terrible, which a: greatly reduced his tip and b: made me doubt every single thing that he told me on the tour. I mean, if he could be so blatantly wrong about that, how can I trust any of his other so called "facts." After all, it was critically acclaimed at the time, and still holds a solid 90% fresh rating on Rotten Tomatoes, and did quite well in ticket sales. It only cost 5 million dollars which is insane when you look at it. This film looks considerably more expensive, and it's crazy to compare to *Looker*, which I mentioned ran around 12 million bucks, and this was made for less than half of that. I mean, you'll also be in disbelief when you see the awesome horse head monsters.

Gaze on these giant lego pieces and know how well they spent that budget to make everything look that good. But when it was released, it went to #1 and eventually grossed $36 million, making it a certified hit. For a while there was an attempt to make a sequel, back in 1996, and would have featured the original cast. But, by then, both David Rappaport and Tiny Ross had died, and when Jack Purvis passed away while they were in the planning stages, they decided to set it aside.

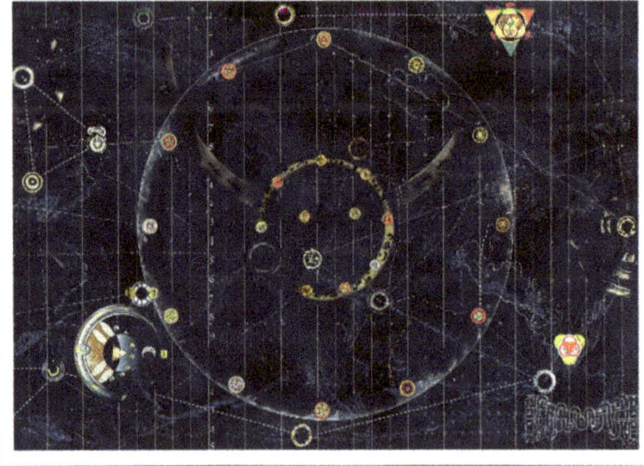

132

My Rating - 5. Without a doubt, this is one my all time favorite movies that's not horror related. This is a rare treat. Not only is it a fun film that feels like a truly epic adventure, but it's also very well made and carefully crafted, and is also oddly philosophical. I don't want to spoil the ending here, but the amount of existential dread that it's given me over the years can't be measured, and how many films that were made for children can you say that about? It's unusual to have something like this that can make you think just as much as it makes you laugh. Oh, and one last thing: I'm not a fan of movies that have a little kid character in the forefront because they're usually written obnoxiously and not well acted, but Craig Warnock walks that fine line expertly.

Cultural Significance - **4.** Again, I may be giving this a little bit of preferential treatment here, but I tend to think that this one is fairly influential. It has a huge roster of names attached to it, a Monty Python connection, and was a decent hit, but it's just never reached the blockbuster status I would hope it would.

Should You Watch It? Yep. It's about time.

Sequel? Sadly, no.

Remake? Yes. In 2024, a TV series was released from Taika Waititi and Jemaine Clement for Apple+. It ran 10 episodes and follows the same basic story as the film, and features Lisa Kudrow and Charlene Yi, although the Bandits are no longer solely little people.

Dec 18th, '81
HEARTBEEPS

Speaking of movies that were meant as family fare, but ended being traumatizing, on December 18, one week before Christmas, *Heartbeeps* was released. And this is a weird one. Really weird. It starts in a robot factory with Cousin Eddie (Randy Quaid) and Baron Harkonnen (Kenneth McMillan) with a robot Latka (Andy Kaufman) who is in

the shop for repairs. While there, he meets the Jerk's wife (Bernadette Peterson), who is also a robot, and they start an unusual romance. There's also this other robot called the Crimebuster that's sort of a mutated Dalek, but it's a bit faulty and blows up bunny rabbits. Then, there's a stand up comic robot called Catskil that's in to fix its one liners. The three robots decide to go out on their own on a fact finding mission and have to sneak past Mr. Futterman (Dick Miller), and his character here is referred to as Walter, so I'm assuming that he's Walter Paisley of course. The Crimebuster overhears them looking for the robots and activates itself to go looking for them, and the good bots use the random parts in their truck to build a tiny one, like a little kid that they named Philco. The factory team is searching for them as well, leading to what you would think would be shenanigans, but I think they move a little too slow to qualify. And this was from Allan Arkush, who had come up in the industry working with Roger Corman doing music videos and had made a splash with *Rock and Roll High School*. This was his first big budget feature film, and he didn't adjust well. It seems like his low key directing style and slow pacing was driving the cast and crew mad, who wanted things to move quicker. Originally, the part of Aqua was intended for Sigourney Weaver, and she wanted to work with Kaufman so it looked like she might sign on, but was persuaded to pass on it, so they moved on to Peters. They did manage to get small roles in there for Mary Woronov, Paul Bartel, and Christopher Guest though.

Meanwhile, Kaufman only took the role as a contingency. Seems he wanted to make a film about his alter ego, Tony Clifton. He pitched the idea to Universal, but since he had only done TV up until this point, they were nervous about giving him his own film. So, they told him that if took this role, and could carry the movie, they would green light the Clifton film. They would rather take their chances with him on this, considering that due to *Star Wars*, market testing showed that anything geared towards kids with robots would be a success. However, when the film bombed, they ended up passing on the Clifton story altogether, something that annoyed the

comic quite a bit. To add to the drama, this film was also affected by a SAG shutdown. They had started shooting in June, but the strike went through in July, causing them to have to cease filming all the way until October. That was for the better anyway, since it meant not filming in the heat, as the prosthetics the actors had to wear were stifling, and would also melt. Kaufman, famous for being difficult, caused some issued on set as well, as since Arkush moved so slowly, Andy would get bored and cause trouble. There also appeared to be some studio meddling, since the original script was meant to be more satirical, but after the producer's input and Arkush's touches, it ended up being drastically watered down. It was overwhelmingly negatively received and has a 0% rating on Rotten Tomatoes

and managed to avoid being nominated for any Razzies, but got 6 nominations from a similar ceremony called The Stinkers Bad Movie Awards, but didn't win any. Kaufman hated the movie, and apologized for it on Letterman, saying that he would personally refund anyone who paid to go see it. It flopped on release, as stated earlier, bringing in only 2 million dollars against a 12 million budget. The only bright side was that Stan Winston's robot makeups were well received and ended up getting an Oscar nomination for Best Makeup, but ended up losing out to *An American Werewolf in London*.

My Rating - 3. This probably doesn't deserve a 3. It's really not a good movie. I may have had an appreciation for this when I was younger, but it absolutely does not hold up. Kaufman, in particular, give the kind of grating performance that makes it hard to see him as any sort of sympathetic character. Peters, however, completely understood the assignment and truly delivers on seeming like a robot, and yet also comes off as distinctly human. But, I have to admit, there's just something about this that draws me in and entertains me. Perhaps it's the whole "train wreck" aspect of it all, but if I come across it, I usually end up watching the whole thing. It's not a good story and the comedy for the most part doesn't land, and it also just sort of ends in a way that resolves the central storylines without actually resolving anything, but even with all that, I get a minor kick out of it.

Cultural Significance - 2.5. I suppose this is a little known, since it did get a healthy amount of cable run time back in the day and it was nominated for an Academy Award. Plus, it has more name actors attached than you'd expect from Heartbeeps, but it's a cult film that never reached mainstream status and just didn't have any sort of influence.

Should You Watch It? I'd actually say yes, but mainly to check out those cool Stan Winston effects.

Sequel? No.

Remake? No

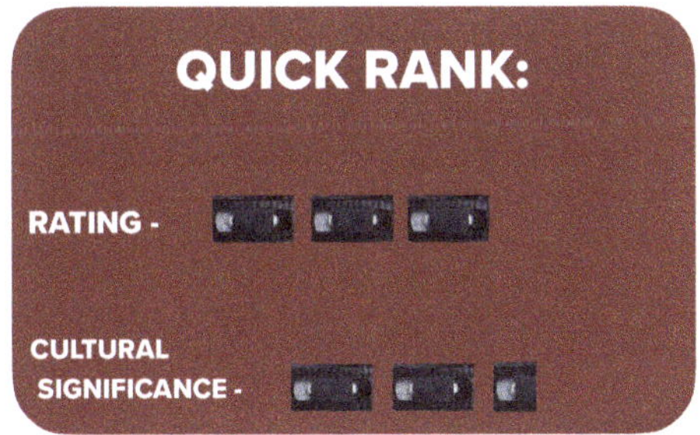

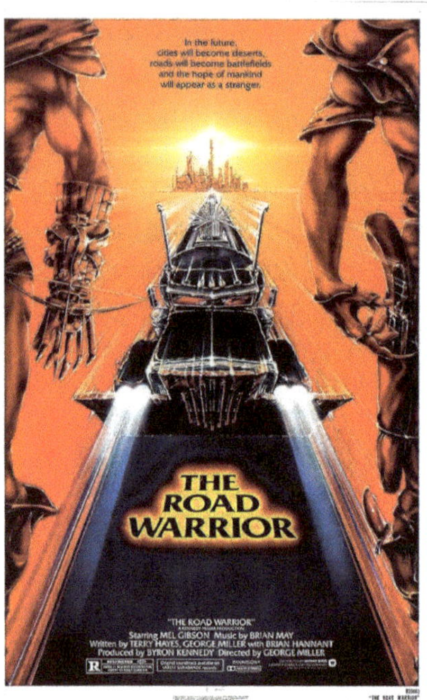

THE ROAD WARRIOR

Get ready for the wasteland to change, because on December 24th in Australia, we got the release of *Mad Max 2*, although it was released here in the states in May of 1982 as *The Road Warrior*. It begins by telling us about a massive decline that destroyed civilization, leading to a shortage of gasoline which ended up in a sort of road war. We get a recap of the events of the first film, and then get Sugartits (Mel Gibson), driving along with his dog, battling it out with marauders. One of them is Wez (Vernon Wells), who took a bit of time off from bugging Gary and Wyatt. Max comes across the Gyro Captain (Bruce Spence) who promises to lead him to an oil refinery, and they're besieged by the gang members. And seriously, can we get a round of applause for the acting skills of that dog? It gives what is likely the most amazing animal performance of all time. Max sees that anyone that tries to leave the refinery is attacked and killed, but he's able to save one and return him to his people, gaining entry. However, when the man dies, they plan to steal Max's car and kick him out, but the marauders show up, led by the hockey mask clad Lord Humongous. One of the inhabitants of the refinery is a young feral kid who has a razor sharp boomerang, and he and

Max bond pretty quickly. The settlement is given a deadline before they're leveled and killed, so Max comes up with a plan to get them out of there while scoring himself some gas. And of course, this was a sequel to the cult hit film *Mad Max*, and directed by a returning George Miller. After the first film was a hit, he had a number of offers and tried to get a rock and roll film called *Roxanne* off the ground, but that never happened. Instead, he was offered a larger budget to return to the world of *Max* and make a sequel. Since he made the first film under quite a bit of scrutiny and had little say in the final product, he relished the idea or going back to that world with more control…and money. So he dove in, with Mel Gibson returning to play Rockatansky. Now, keep in mind that *Mad Max*, the original film, was not a big hit in the US, and at this

point no one really knew who Gibson was. In fact, for the first film, the trailers didn't even really show him, instead focusing on the action sequences in the film. So when it came time for a sequel, they realized that it still wasn't that well known. Because of this, instead of calling it *Mad Max 2*, the title in Australia, they changed the name to simply *The Road Warrior,* and acted as if it were the first film in the franchise. One snippet regarding the original to this one is that the character of Lord Humongous may have been conceived of as being Max's former partner, Goose. In the original, Goose was a cop with a bit of a brutal streak, who is then attacked and burnt alive by a gang member. He survives but is unrecognizable and his ultimate fate is never mentioned. Early on in the process for *Mad Max 2*, it's rumored that the idea was that Goose would return as the main villain, but they eventually dropped the idea, and just left in hints, indicating that it could still possibly be meant to be him under that mask. He's clearly burnt up, and they use vehicles and weapons that are police issued, so it's a possible interpretation, although has never been confirmed. Speaking of Humongous, considering that this was released in late '81, there's the slight possibility that his mask could have had some sort of influence on a certain summer camp stalker. It's never actually been acknowledged, but the timeline does fit, so it's certainly possible, but who knows? When it was released, it was a bit hit, both in Australia and the rest of the world. It doubled the original's take Down Under and pulled in almost $24 million in the US, compared to its budget of just under $5 million. Oddly, over here, it became way more known than its predecessor and most people had this as their first experience with the character, to the point that when they put out *Mad Max* on video, they basically marketed it like a prequel. It was also critically acclaimed, and has been both referred to as one of the best action films of all time, as well as a sequel that far outdoes the original, and won a number of Aussie film awards.

"AND THE ROAD WARRIOR? THAT WAS THE LAST WE EVER SAW OF HIM. HE LIVES NOW... ONLY IN MY MEMORIES."

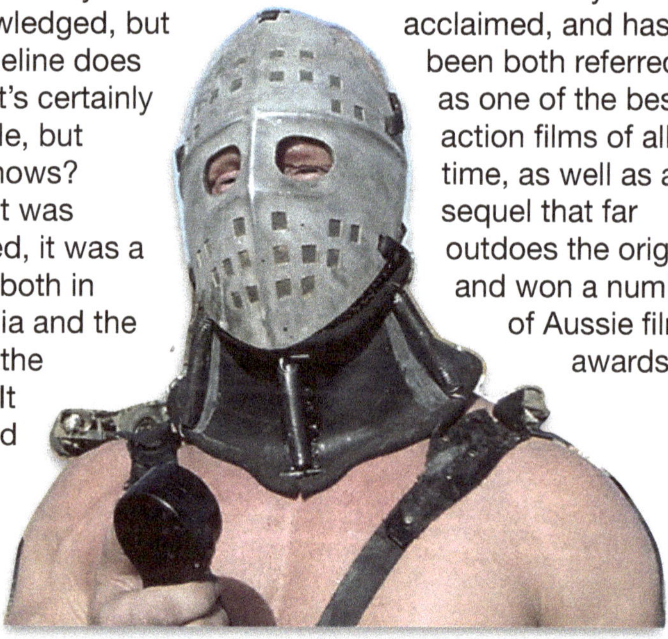

My Rating - 4.5. When I think of solid action films, this is the first thing that my mind goes to. This entire movie is essentially one long chase scene from one side of the desert to the another and then back again, and I'm here for it. It doesn't feel the need to get complicated with lore and overstuff it with characters. Hell, you could accuse it of having very little in the way of actual character. Even Max is basically just a guy who does some stuff. He doesn't have this big arc that he follows and develops as a person. And I'm not saying that as a negative. This movie doesn't need that because it's telling you right up from that this is a white knuckle roller coaster ride. That's why I can't take some of the criticism that came with *Fury Road* about how Max is sidelined in favor of the other characters, which makes me think that those people have never actually bothered to see this movie, where Max is more or less a side character.

Cultural Significance - 5. When I did the video version, I gave this a 4.5 and said that the reason it didn't get a full 5 is because it was a sequel, and some of that relevance goes to the original, but I've changed my mind, since this was how most people met the franchise, as opposed to the first one. And the impact it had was tremendous. Later volumes of the Project will show that as all the imitators start to arrive.

Should You Watch It? Yes, but don't forget to buckle up.

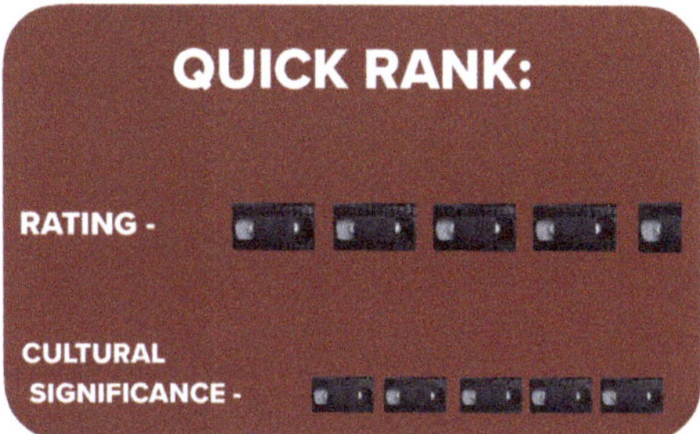

Sequel? Yes.
Mad Max Beyond Thunderdome would arrive a few years later, and then much later on, the saga would continue with *Fury Road* and *Furiosa*.

Remake? No.

QUICK RANK:

RATING -

CULTURAL SIGNIFICANCE -

Dec 25th, '81

MODERN PROBLEMS

Our last entry with a known date arrived on Christmas Day, back in the US with *Modern Problems*. It gives us a group of air traffic controllers and one is Fletch (Chevy Chase), and kicks into a theme song that lives rent free in my head. Chase's Max finds out his insane jealousy has caused his girlfriend to leave him, so he consults Loretta Haggers (Mary Kay Place), and then runs into his old friend Brian (Brian Doyle Murray), and by this point, this is probably the closest that Chevy Chase would be able to get to Bill Murray. Side note: Brian Doyle Murray has crafted a solid career for himself without ever just being known as Bill's brother. He's taken care of by Nell and yeah, I can refer to her as her most famous role, but that would also just be Nell (Nell Carter). One of Brian's clients is Jack Glack (Dabney Coleman), and after driving back from his party, Max ends up behind a truck full of toxic waste that splashes onto him. Instead of becoming a hideously deformed creature of superhuman size and strength, he glows and the next morning seems to move objects with his mind. He uses it for petty revenge against the guy that Darcy is now dating, and tries to use his powers to win her back, which includes almost killing a random ballet dancer. It leads to a weekend getaway at Brian's place at the beach as Max unleashes his powers against everyone, particularly Winslow, who is attempting to steal Darcy. This was a staple of HBO back in the day and was cowritten and directed by Ken Shapiro, who had worked with Chase on a movie called *The Groove Tube*, a collection of shorts and sketches. This was technically his first feature film, which Chevy noted caused issues on set due to Shapiro's inexperience, but says he thinks they made a good film. The experience didn't exactly wow the director either, and he disliked the corporate structure of the studio world and left the industry after this film. Most of the ending took place on sound stages, but for the exteriors, they used something that may look familiar. And it was the real *Psycho* house from the Universal Studio back lot tour, although there's some dispute. There's a website that details the history of the house on the lot and says it was dismantled in 198, and theoretically transported to for use in the film, but

elsewhere, a historian did a comparison of the features, along with the proportions and determined that it appears to be a replica. It was released with a PG rating, which upset the writers, as there were originally more raunchy moments included, and they felt some of the best parts were removed. When it was released, they skipped a critic screening, which is usually a sign the studios think it'll get torn apart. If they think a film will get bad reviews and discourage viewers from going, they'll not show it in advance. Critics still review it, but they'll have to do so after the film is released, and by that time, the movie's had its opening weekend and hopefully done good numbers. And their tactic worked because, well, it DID get bad reviews, but still did solid business. The budget was $8 million and it brought in a little over $26, marking it as a decent success, if not exactly a blockbuster.

My Rating - 3. I really thought my rating on this would be higher. I have some pretty fond memories of it from when it was on cable, but it just does not manage to live up to them. It could be because my general opinion of Chase has dropped, both as a performer and as a person, but I also just didn't enjoy the film as much as I would have thought. There are some funny bits and when it gets to the mayhem of the ending, it clicks, but holy crap, does it take forever to get to them.

Cultural Significance - 3. This is a tough one here, because I feel like this is fairly well remembered since it was on a constant cable rotation throughout the '80s, so it definitely deserves some sort of significance. Plus, it has a number of known names, including Chase himself, who was certainly a bigger draw at on point. However, I also think that it's notoriety has faded since then, and once it wasn't featured on regular screenings, people seemed to forget about it.

Should You Watch It? Sure, there's still some great bits, but be prepared for some filler in between them.

Sequel? No.

Remake? No

QUICK RANK:

RATING -

CULTURAL SIGNIFICANCE -

???, '81
SEX IS CRAZY

We're now entering the territory of films that didn't have a confirmed release date, but this one was known that it came out sometime in '81 in Spain and it's *Sex is Crazy*. It involves aliens kidnapping Earth women to impregnate them and their race has rapid natal periods, so they can have a baby every 8 seconds, but it's all just a show where the audience is wearing masks? What's going on here? It's then this stream of consciousness thing with secret agents, microfilm, and of course a variety of sexual shenanigans, but don't expect outright pornography here. This is strictly softcore stuff. And there's plenty of it. But, anyway, the director here is Jess Franco, and this is already the 4th film of his that I've covered on the Project : two in 1980 and two so far in 1981. Seeing as how the guy has 207 movies to his name, I'll probably have to cover a lot more. This one gets surreal when the characters we're following are made to simply be characters in a movie, and we often see the crew, with Franco himself as the director, so it blurs the line of fantasy and reality, and for most of it, it's just this weird tale of these two couples and tons of hormones, but then at like the one hour mark, we find out that actual aliens have seen the stage play and think it's a good idea and now want to use humans to breed. There's very little plot going on, and a number of nonsensical moment, like a bit where our two protagonists are in a car and just start speaking in gibberish to each other. It's absurd to the point that you have to wonder if there really was any sort of message or meaning here or if it was just some inspired madness.

My Rating - 2. I have a complicated relationship with Franco in that I don't like around 90% of what he's made. But this is perhaps one of the more tolerable examples, even if it's still pretty damn dull. On the plus side, though, there's a good deal of comedy that actually lands here, and I do respect the completely off the cuff nature of it all. But at some point, you realize that you're just watching weird for the sake of being weird, and even if it really is trying to say something, what it's trying to say isn't very compelling.

Cultural Significance - 1. WIth the exception of one or two movies, most of Franco's films have failed to really make a mark, and this is no exception, even if it's one of his more surreal entries.

Should You Watch It? I would say no, unless you really have a soft spot for stream of consciousness sex comedies.

Sequel? No.

Remake? No

???, '81
LIFEPOD

We now jump to another one that has an unknown date, but it's *Lifepod*, not to be confused with 1993's *Lifepod*, and this has an ad for a ship going to Jupiter with a trademark in 2191, so we're in the far future. That shuttle is on its maiden voyage, but there's an emergency and they have to abandon ship. People get away on various lifepods, but some of the crew are still on board. We meet Simmons (Joe Perry), who meets up with Fiona, played by Kristine DeBell, who was in *Meatballs, Tag the Assassination Game* and *A Talking Cat?*, but of course IMDB lists her most known film as the one X-rated movie she did. They end up finding a group of others who are still there as well, and have to try to find their way to a lifepod, and oh my god, is that freaking M.A.N.T.I.S (Carl Lumbly)? It is! There's this sort of robot thing with a laser on it keeping them in line, and there's a secret passage that they're able to use to get to a pod, but the captain stays behind, and the ship's computer is trying to convince them to come back. And our director here is Bruce Bryant, and it's the only thing he's ever directed, although he has a considerable amount of work in other aspects in the industry and seems to have found his niche in TV title sequences. He's done the opening title graphics for shows like *Frasier, Roseanne*, and *Cheers*. This was one of a whole bunch of super cheap sci-fi flicks pumped out in this era by producer Robert Emenegger, who did *The Killings at Outpost Zero* around this same time, and just tried to get as many inexpensive genre flicks out as could in a short time span. And yeah, after the first like, 15 minutes with them hustling to get onto the lifepod, it then just sorta goes into this whole "nothing much happens" mode as everyone just sits around talking for a while, and by a while, i mean, like the next hour.

My Rating - 1.5. Wow. This is just a snoozer. The initial setup seems to have some promise, to have some promise, but it absolutely never delivers on any of it. It turns into shot after shot of people walking down corridors and sitting in rooms, talking. If they had tried to produce this as a short as part of a sci-fi anthology, it could have worked, but it's just not enough story to stretch into a 90 minute format.

Cultural Significance - 1. Mark this one down as another one that's nearly completely forgotten and doesn't feature much in the way of recognizable faces. Plus, if you try to look it up, most of the links lead to the '93 version.

Should You Watch It? Skip this one unless you're having a party and it's getting late and you want your guests to leave.

Sequel? No.

Remake? No. The '93 version is a completely different story and isn't related.

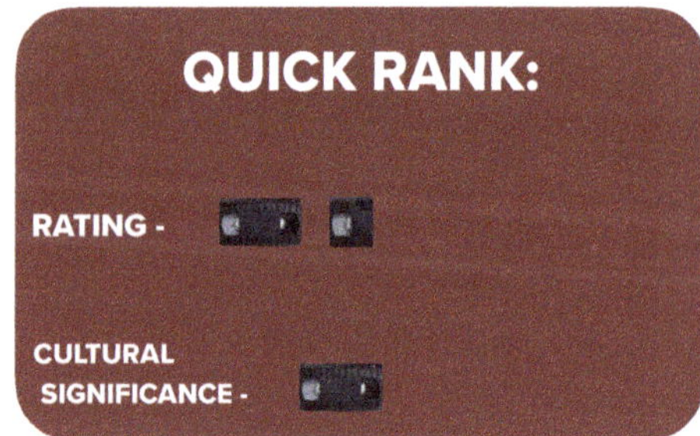

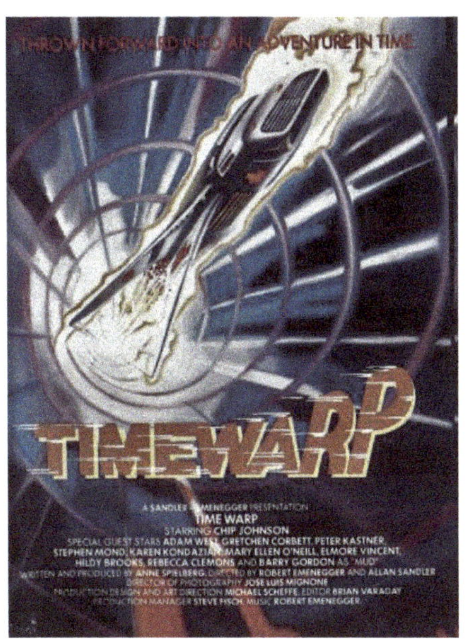

???, '81

TIMEWARP

Continuing on with entries with an unknown release date and it's kind of funny that we've talked about Rocky Horror so much just a few entries ago and then there's this movie called *Timewarp*. In it, there's an astronaut on his way back from a space mission which they say took him to the further regions of the galaxy. The Colonel overseeing it all is a Caped Crusader (Adam West), and the astronaut's wife is Gretchen Corbett, who we saw not that long ago in *Jaws of Satan*, and her kid is Robbie (Steven Mond) and this was his last film. I guess he did that run on *Diff'rent Strokes* and then just left the industry. Captain Devore was said to have been in space for one year, and when asked what sustained him through the loneliness he has a simple reply: sex. The Colonel is trying to steal his wife, since he thinks that the Captain is just a silly, silly man. He's super aggressive and handsy, like, back off bro, but the problems really arise when Mark enters into a field of energy as he's approaching earth. It has some sort of effect and he loses two days, but when he lands the ship there's no one there to greet him, and no one seems to see him. His robot companion theorizes that they went through a time warp and they're out of phase with their own dimension, and are one year out of place. Because of that, he's invisible to other people, and was reported to have died on the way home. So, in that very last entry, I talked about Robert Emenegger, who produced a whole bunch of low budget sci-fi movies over a short amount of time to have this package of films. It included *Killings at Outpost Zeta* and *Lifepod*, and this is another one. The biggest difference between this one and his other projects appears to be trying to inject humor into this one, even if it mostly doesn't work. Now, there's very little information about this out there, but all of his films were made as part of a sort of syndication packet for TV airings, and it's listed as a TV movie, even if there's no confirmation about where or when it aired.

My Rating - 2. This is a step in the right direction, mainly because watching West ham it up is always a treat, and he's in fine form here. However, just like Lifepod, this is basically just twenty minutes of story stretched out to ninety, with a heaping helping of filler thrown in to pad it out.

Cultural Significance - 1. You can basically just copy and paste my comments about *Lifepod* right here. No one knows what this is, and it never really led into anything else.

Should You Watch It? This is an easy pass.

Sequel? No.

Remake? No

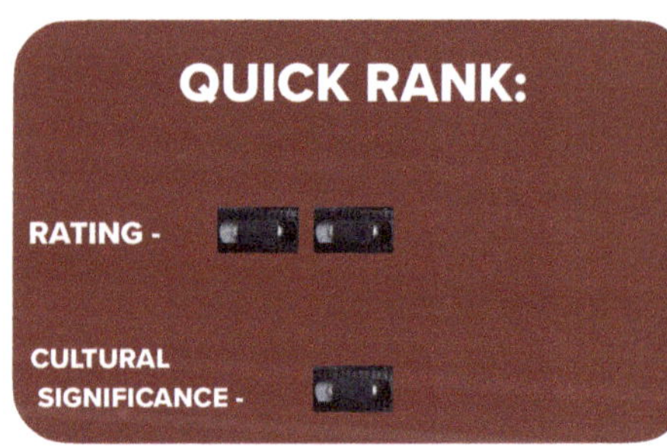

THE PERFECT WOMAN

Speaking of Emenegger, another film with an unknown date, very similar to *Timewarp* is *The Perfect Woman*. It leads off telling us about an alien king named King Kroger, on the hunt for a perfect woman in order to produce an heir. Cameron Mitchell is here since he didn't just do crappy action films around this time, he also did crappy sci-fi. The king is Buck Laughlin (Fred Willard) and this may be off the subject a little bit, but let's take a guess at how much he can bench press. Come on, what do you think? So, if the king doesn't produce an offspring, his cousin will take over the throne from him and they don't like him because they say he's a sissy. Kroger declares that his wife come from Earth, since he's obsessed with our TV shows and enlists two of his people to go find her. One of them (Barry Gordon) may not look familiar, but he'll likely sound familiar, as he's mostly known for his voice. He's the voice of Donatello on the entire run of the original *Turtles* cartoon, and in a bunch of *Turtles* games. So, Zig and Emo head to earth and begin their search, advertising with that Gomer Pyle guy (Ronnie Schell) who, coincidentally has also a massive amount of voice work in cartoons. And yeah, everything that I said about *Timewarp* or *Lifepod* applies here. This is another of that package of quick and cheap films that Emenegger put together. Now, he didn't direct all of them but he did do this and *Timewarp*, although this one had a co director in Allan Sandler, who basically just worked with Emenegger on this set of flicks and didn't do much else. Like *Timewarp*, there's just not much information out there about this one, and like that film, was made for TV although it's also not exactly clear where or when it played, although it's assumed that it actually did at one point. The saddest part about it is that it manages to have Fred Willard in it and then essentially just sidelines him for 80 percent of the film. To be fair, he wasn't really that well known as a comic actor at this point. Sure, he had done some funny stuff previously, but that was mixed in with more serious work. I mean, the guy was in *Salem's Lot* not long before this, so it's not like everyone just saw him and said: "comedy only."

My Rating - 1.5. Another dud from this group of films. This is boring and not funny in the slightest, but at least had a couple of moments I thought were fun.

Cultural Significance - 1. You can basically just copy and paste my comments about *Lifepod* and *Timewarp* right here. No one knows what this is, and it never really led into anything else.

Should You Watch It? Only if you want to see Fred Willard not doing things that you know Fred Willard for.

Sequel? No.

Remake? No

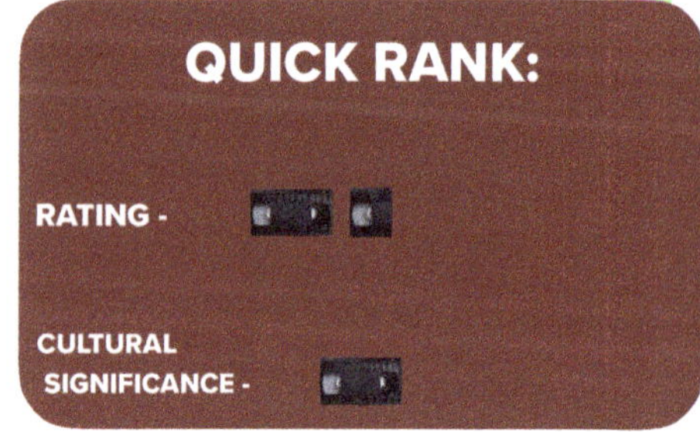

WARP SPEED

Are we really doing this? I guess we're doing this, because this next one also does not have a confirmed date, and just came out some time in 1981 and it's *Warp Speed*. It has Dr.Trask who has psychic powers and is part of a space mission. They're sent up to investigate the return of a ship called the Atlas. It seems that it went missing a while back, and has now just returned. They board it and find a video message from the previous crew all killing each other and just say "we're leaving"…wait. Different movie. Instead, Trask enters the ship and the plan is for her to use her abilities to merge with the memory imprints that remain on the Atlas to find out what happened there. She witnesses the events, showing people killing each other and she sees one of Gotham's finest (Adam West again), and i guess he's popular here this year, but he's thankfully playing this one a bit more serious than he was in *Timewarp*. And hey, Barry Gordon is in this too, so this seems to be a pretty small pool of actors between these three movies. If you guessed that this was another of the films from that Emenegger bundle of quickie sci-fi flicks, then you'll be 100% right. He only served as a producer on this one, though, but did also do the music for it. It was directed by Allan Sandler, on his own for this one, but based on the previous two, don't get your hopes up. So, Trask basically watches as the morale degrades amongst the crew and they start to turn on each other, but also sees like, fever dream weddings. It all gets a touch surreal, with a fluffy space horse or whatever that thing was supposed to be, as the doc tries to figure out just what happened. She sure as hell takes her damn sweet time, because like *Timewarp* and *The Perfect Woman*, it's sort of like they had enough concepts for a half hour story. Basically, they had enough for a *Twilight Zone* episode, but then padded everything out so it hit feature length. It's like they had access to this space ship set and a handful of actors for a few days and just put them in that set and fed them lines with no clear direction or plot and timed it and as soon as they hit 90 minutes worth were like, "TIME!" And to make matters worse, there's no finale to this film. If you're waiting for a climactic finish, this one is like, nah. It's just gonna end.

My Rating - 1.5. It's partially a little interesting to see West take things more seriously and actually give a performance, but there's just not enough here for him to sink his teeth into and without one or two intriguing bits, this is a total waste of time.

Cultural Significance - 1. You can basically just copy and paste my comments about *Lifepod, Timewarp,* and *The Perfect Woman* right here. No one knows what this is, and it never really led into anything else.

Should You Watch It? Are you seeing a pattern with the Emenegger stuff? Pass.

Sequel? No.

Remake? No

Alright. Here's another one, and oh man. This is Escape From DS-3 and it's another one from Robert Emenegger. And I quit. This is not what i signed up for. There's only so much I can write about these things. So, what's this one "about"? We have a guy named Lavette who is framed for a crime and put on trial and he's played by Jackson Bostwick, no relation to Barry Bostwick. This guy was the original Shazam, or Captain Marvel as the character is actually known as, even if DC's not really supposed to promote that anymore. Anyway, he was that character for the first season of the *Shazam* show back in the '70s but was fired and replaced two episodes into the second season because he was injured on set and had to have it taken care of. The producers then claimed that he was trying to negotiate for higher pay as the reasoning for the firing. He sued them over it and won, getting a pay out for his remaining episodes, but his career never really rebounded. So, Lavette gets sentenced to a space super prison where Hightower (Bubba Smith) is also serving, and I guess they have some robotic sexbots on board for the prisoners, so it's made to not seem that bad. Mac says they have legal drugs, sexbots and entertainment, so yeah, not seeming that terrible a sentence, I suppose. But nope, because the authorities there are abusive, of course, and an actor from *Warp Speed* is in this too and I didn't mention this there, but he's Cameron Mitchell Jr. Yep that's right, he's Cameron Mitchell's son. They then begin the very long and slow process of planning their escape by sitting around rooms and talking and then talking in other rooms, and if the sets look familiar, it's because they're using the same spaceship that they used for *Warp Speed* since it was all about using that low budget as much as possible. Of course, it should be obvious by now that this is just another of that package of low budget sci fi syndication movies that I've covered here and hope to never discuss again, because thank goodness that this is the final one and the next couple of entires are by other people, and I never have to type the name Emenegger again.

My Rating - 1.5. The only reason that this one is saved from getting a single tape is the presence of Bubba Smith, who is charming and gives a solid performance. Otherwise, it's just as flaccid As the several I talked about before.

Cultural Significance - 1. You can basically just copy and paste my comments about *Lifepod, Timewarp, The Perfect Woman,* and *Warp Speed* right here. No one knows what this is, and it never really led into anything else.

Should You Watch It? You should have figured it out by now. If you see Mr. E's name…run.

Sequel? No.

Remake? No

???. '81
GUNDALA

We're moving away from that drudgery on to another part of the world for a film with no confirmed date, but one that came out in 1981, and possibly in September in Indonesia. I promise it's not another Emenegger film, and it's *Gundala* or I guess, *Gundala Putra Petir*. It's from Indonesia, and this might get tricky because I couldn't quite find a subtitled version but found the movie on YouTube and used the auto translate closed caption, so we'll see how this goes. It starts with some criminals doing a drop and then killing their messenger, and then we have a doctor with some fluid that appears to be Herbert West's ReAgent? He shoots himself up with it, which..come on man, you're either getting a Hyde or a Green Goblin or something that way. He then electrocutes himself. On purpose. And then, you know how awkward the birthday song is as you just sit there while people sing. Now imagine that multiplied by six because that's what happens here. They sing a happy birthday song. Six freaking times. Sancoko misses his lady friend's party to do his experiment, which by the way, is an anti lightning serum that makes you resistant to electricity? I mean, the odds of being struck by lightning is about 1 in 15,300, so I'm not sure it's the most useful or wise way to spend your inventing time. But how about this for circumstance? That night, he's hit by lighting, so it's a good thing he injected that damn serum. But no, it's not just any lightning. It's from the King of Lightning, a silver clad gentleman with some killer facial hair. He imbues Sancoko with supernatural powers and a kickass suit with winged ears and is given a magic necklace, along with the name Gundala. He busts into action to save a little girl and has his very own theme song, and this is based on an actual comic book hero of the same name. His comic debuted in Indonesia back in 1969, and the word Gundala is a play on the Javanese word for lightning, gundolo. It's said that the original character was greatly influenced by the spate of American superheroes coming out at that time, and I think that his powers were meant to be lightning based, but for most of the film, he's simply portrayed as very fast and acrobatic. It's kind of unclear if he even has powers, or has simply been made a badass fighter. Like, he even stabs a guy with a switchblade at one point. It's hard to find out if the film was successful over there, and it wasn't really released in the states, but it was the first Indonesian superhero film based on one of their comics. I should point out that he actually DOES use lightning powers in the very tail end of the film, which was apparently as much as the budget would allow.

My Rating - 3. After the last assortment of films, I really needed something like this. Watching it gave me throwback vibes to those classic '70s Spider-Man TV movies or the Captain America ones, and I mean that in the best sense as well as the worst. It shares some of the weaknesses of those as well, and tends to be really slow in the middle of it all. The biggest thing holding it back is the money aspect because the beginning really sets up all this electrical lightning stuff, but then they have to put all of that on the back burner to show Gundala doing some stabbing instead. They finally figure it all out and give you what you want to see in the finale, but by then it's maybe a little too late. Even with that, it's still a fun ride, and it's certainly doing the best with what little resources that it has. Plus, I don't know, maybe I've always been a fool for superheroes with wings on their ears.

Cultural Significance - **1.** This one sure was a hit in Indonesia, but it's extremely unknown here. In the US, *Gundala* is Gundalost.

Should You Watch It? Sure. It's some good old fashioned silly superhero fun.

Sequel? No.

Remake? Yes. In 2019, there was a remake simply called Gundala that had the hopes of kicking off a new cinematic universe over there, and this version had lightning powers throughout. Two other films did follow, both featuring an appearance by the character, and there's currently 6 others planned.

We start this one off with a bit of a disputed release date, although it's known to have come out in 1981. Some state February 12th, but that's unconfirmed and it's *Escape From Galaxy 3*, although known as *Star Crash 2*. There's a space princess, played by Sherry Buchanan who we recognize from *Zombie*

Holocaust, as well as *Tentacles.* When an unknown ship enters their territory they realize that it's most likely Oraclon, a space warlord, and prepare for the end. They're right, and Oraclon and his sparkly beard are there to take over, leading to frantic space battles. The king sends away Belle Star in the care of his most trusted man, Lithan, while garbed in the most ridiculous outfits and funkified music. This is some top notch disco space adventure. Belle's outfit takes the cake though, for being completely impractical It covers one boob and the other has a little star pasty thing going on, but then it's like, she only gets coverage for one leg and one butt cheek. I guess it's the equivalent of when you're in bed and you have to have one leg under the covers and one leg out. I mean, are they in space or in the Ice Capades? They land on an Earth-like planet, and what's funny is that up until this point, about 40 minutes in or so, this could very easily be misconstrued

as a kids movie. But then there's an extended scene for Belle Star frolicking naked in a waterfall, and from that point on, it just becomes ground zero for horniness. The director on this is listed as being Ben Norman although that was a pseudonym for Bitto Albertini, and most of his work was either in the Italian gladiator flicks or erotic films, including several *Emmanuelle* movies. The funny thing is though, that if you go to IMDB, it also lists Luigi Cozzi as a director. Now, Luigi has already been in the Project with the horror flick, *Contamination* in 80, but in 1978 he made a sci fi *Star Wars* knock off called *Star Crash* that's pretty damn fun. But Cozzi didn't really have anything to do with this one at all, but a large amount of the special effects from *Star Crash* are recycled here. In fact, almost all of the models and miniatures are just lifted out of that movie and inserted in this one. And weirdly, Cozzi did try to make a sequel of his own to *Star Crash* and wasn't able to really get it going, mainly due to rights issues and writers falling out. And yeah, this one has no crashing stars and barely has any escaping from Galaxy 3. Most of it is sort of a weird series of sexual tension to the point that you wonder if this was an adult film script that they decided at the last minute to not have any actual adult content and just a bunch of horny people and occasional boobs. Nothing really happens until the last 15 minutes, when they finally go to face Oraclon with their newfound sex energy, but by then it's a little too late.

My Rating - 1.5. Sadly, I'll have to end this volume on a little bit of a down note, since there's really not much happening in this one. It really tricks you, too, since the opening makes it look like it's going to be this over the top spectacle with the clothing and music. But then, it settles in on that other planet and everything slows down to a crawl. Like I said, it gets back to the silliness at the very end of things, and that's where that extra .5 comes into play, but it's a small consolation for sitting out the previous hour or so.

Cultural Significance - **1.** We're ending on a low note in terms of significance as well, since this one is mostly known for reusing a chunk of the footage from a more impactful and much more entertaining film. Beyond that, it's not even one that's talked out from a "so bad, it's good" aspect, since it never even reaches that point.

Should You Watch It? Not really. The outfits sure are something to see, though.

Sequel? No.

Remake? No

INDEX

A

I

The Incredible Shrinking Woman (rating 3.5, SFCS 3, total score = 6.5) - pgs 79-81

L

The Last Chase (rating 2, SFCS 2, total score = 4) - pgs 84-86
The Lathe of Heaven (rating 4, SFCS 2, total score = 6) - pgs 6-8
Lifepod (rating 1.5, SFCS 1, total score 2.5) - pgs 147-148
Looker (rating 4, SFCS 3.5, total score = 7.5) - pgs 124-126

M

Modern Problems (rating 3, SFCS 3, total score = 6) - pgs 142-144

O

Outland (rating 3.5, SFCS 3, total score = 6.5) - pgs 93-95

P

The Perfect Woman (rating 1.5, SFCS 1, total score = 2.5) - pgs 151-152
Pumaman (rating 2.5, SFCS 1.5, total score = 4) - pgs 12-14

R

The Return (rating 2, SFCS 2, total score = 4) - pgs 74-75
The Road Warrior (rating 4.5, SFCS 5, total score = 9.5) - pgs 138-141

S

Saturn 3 (rating 3.5, SFCS 3.5, total score = 7) - pgs 15-18
School in the Crosshairs (rating 3.5, SFCS 1.5, total score = 5) - pgs 106-108
Sex is Crazy (rating 2, SFCS 1, total score = 3) - pgs 145-146
Shock Treatment (rating 3, SFCS 3, total score = 6) - 127-129
Simon (rating 2.5, SFCS 2.5, total score = 5) - pgs 19-21
Super Fuzz (rating 3.5, SFCS 2.5, total score = 6) - pgs 71-73
Superman 2 (rating 4.5, SFCS 4.5, total score = 9) pgs 63-66

T

Threshold (rating 3, SFCS 2, total score = 5) - 117-118
Time Bandits (rating 5, SFCS 4, total score = 9) - pgs 130-133
Timewarp (rating 2, SFCS 1, total score = 3) - pgs 149-150

W

War of the Worlds : Next Century (rating 4, SFCS 2, total score = 6) - pgs 119-121
Warp Speed (rating 1.5, SFCS 1, total score = 2.5) - pgs 153-154

X

Xanadu (rating 3, SFCS 3.5, total score = 6.5) - pgs 46-49

THE AWARDS

BEST EFFECTS - THE EMPIRE STRIKES BACK
BEST "SO BAD, IT'S GOOD" - SUPER FUZZ
MOST WTF - THE FORBIDDEN ZONE
MOST UNIQUE - TIME BANDITS
MOST OVERRATED - SHOCK TREATMENT
MOST UNDERRATED - LOOKER
MOST AMAZING - FLASH GORDON

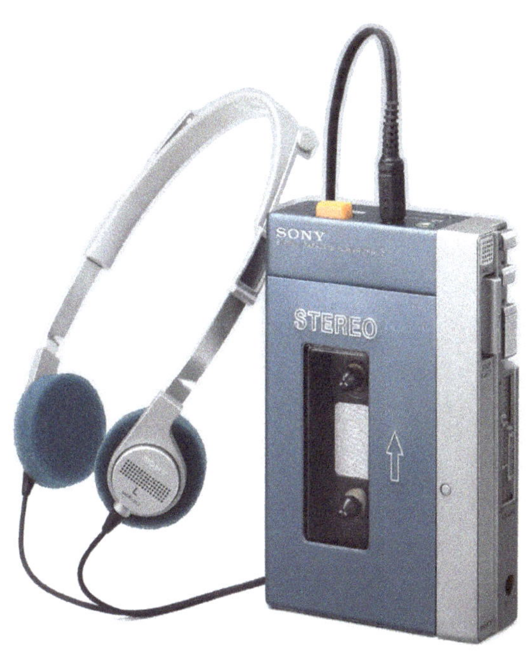